Developing Academic Programs:
The Climate for Innovation

by Daniel T. Seymour

ASHE-ERIC Higher Education Report No. 3, 1988

Prepared by

Clearinghouse on Higher Education
The George Washington University

Published by

Association for the Study of
Higher Education

Jonathan D. Fife,
Series Editor

Cite as
Seymour, Daniel T. *Developing Academic Programs: The Climate for Innovation.* ASHE-ERIC Higher Education Report No. 3. Washington, D.C.: Association for the Study of Higher Education, 1988.

Library of Congress Catalog Card Number 88-83590
ISSN 0884-0040
ISBN 0-913317-46-2

Managing Editor: Christopher Rigaux
Manuscript Editor: Barbara Fishel/Editech
Cover design by Michael David Brown, Rockville, Maryland

The ERIC Clearinghouse on Higher Education invites individuals to submit proposals for writing monographs for the Higher Education Report series. Proposals must include:
1. A detailed manuscript proposal of not more than five pages.
2. A chapter-by-chapter outline.
3. A 75-word summary to be used by several review committees for the initial screening and rating of each proposal.
4. A vita.
5. A writing sample.

ERIC **Clearinghouse on Higher Education**
School of Education and Human Development
The George Washington University
One Dupont Circle, Suite 630
Washington, D.C. 20036-1183

ASHE Association for the Study of Higher Education
Texas A&M University
Department of Educational Administration
Harrington Education Center
College Station, Texas 77843

This publication was prepared partially with funding from the Office of Educational Research and Improvement, U.S. Department of Education, under contract no. ED RI-88-062014. The opinions expressed in this report do not necessarily reflect the positions or policies of OERI or the Department.

EXECUTIVE SUMMARY

In 1663, Harvard College's curriculum contained only six different subjects: political philosophy, ethics, astronomy, geometry, physics, and languages (Latin and Greek). Three hundred years from now, today's academic programs will seem equally as limited. Over the centuries, the core of what we teach in our colleges and universities has changed dramatically. But the ongoing process is a slow evolution. Over several years, a number of new programs are offered, other programs are split, some are merged, and occasionally a program is phased out. The process by which this gradual reshaping occurs involves all aspects of the institution—new faculty members are hired, support services developed, equipment and supplies purchased, brochures reprinted, and buildings constructed. Eventually the entire college or university is transformed. This change should not be left to the vagaries of personal preferences or social fads but rather should be actively designed to support the mission of the institution. Administrators, trustees, and faculty members need to understand how institutions are being transformed in today's environment and how the process of developing new academic programs can be improved for tomorrow.

Several different bodies of research and writings contain *practical* findings useful in the development of new programs. First is innovation—the process, the people, and the product. The literature in the area of organizational theory provides valuable insights into key questions: What are the characteristics associated with successful innovation in organizations? How do these characteristics relate to colleges and universities? The literature on strategic planning provides additional practical findings. Strategic planning does not involve plans as much as it does process. It is a way of thinking. And as such, strategic planning is a useful structure within which decisions—decisions about new academic programs—can be made. Finally, program evaluation is a study using various tools and techniques designed to judge and improve the worth of some educational object. It is this mechanism that in fact ultimately allows us to make value judgments about the strengths and weaknesses of academic programs. The overlap of these three areas—innovation in organizations, strategic planning, and program evaluation—provides the framework for this report.

Are Colleges and Universities Innovative?

Colleges and universities are an enigma: "The university is among the most traditional of all institutions of our society, and, at the same time, it is the institution most responsible for the changes that make our society the most changing in the history of man'' (Hesburgh 1971, p. 3). More than a few higher education institutions have been in continual existence for 500 years. They have proven to be models of adaptability.

But the basic culture and structure of these institutions, while effective in the past, may not be appropriate in a modern society characterized by accelerated change. For example, while the basic decentralized structure of colleges and universities continues to be a source of strength for fostering new ideas in this quickly paced environment, other forces are working to impede innovative change. The fragmentation of departments and disciplines into increasingly specialized units creates an atmosphere of isolation, and stagnation is an obvious consequence of such isolation. The decade between 1985 and 1995 marks the first serious leveling off of enrollments since World War II. Innovations have always been a natural by-product of a growth environment in higher education. Administrators, trying to manage constancy and decline, have not been terribly successful at identifying mechanisms to free up resources for innovative change in the face of retrenchment. And the new wave of accountability at the state and system levels has resulted in additional policies and reporting procedures for numerous measures of assessment, status reports, approval processes for new programs, and so on. While the attention to such evaluation procedures strengthens managerial control, a loss of flexibility, adaptability, and simplicity often accompanies it.

In addition to all of these restrictions, higher education has a high ''comfortability index.'' As an institution, it operates with no great sense of urgency or uncertainty—or discomfort. A climate for innovation is therefore not a natural happenstance. It must be orchestrated.

How Much Has the Development of New Programs Been Studied in the Literature?

Developing new programs falls within a general category of evaluation procedures for academic programs. Historically, research and writing in higher education have concentrated on the use of means to assess the strengths and weaknesses of ongoing programs. The purpose of such assessments, usually in the form of program reviews, has been the improvement of the program's quality. More recently, the emphasis has shifted toward the use of program review as a means to make decisions about the long-run viability of programs and allocation of resources. Program discontinuance, the detailed analysis of an existing program for the purpose of deciding its future in the institution, has also become more heavily studied as scarce resources have forced colleges and universities to retrench.

But studies of new program development have not followed from this attention to program evaluation, and it appears that the development of new programs, as an area of study, is caught in a dilemma. In a growth environment, new programs are a natural by-product of growth and are not perceived to require complex planning. Ideas emerge from the faculty, are supported by the administration or not, go through a standardized approval process, and then become a permanent addition to a college or university's brochure. While program planning has not been seen as very important in a growth environment, it has not been seen as very practical in a no-growth environment. Institutions with high fixed costs, like colleges and universities, find it difficult to generate flexible resources. As highly decentralized institutions, they also find it politically and psychologically difficult to retrench and to innovate simultaneously.

Thus, while the corporate world sees new product development as requisite for its future existence (and, consequently, is intrigued with questions about the source of ideas for new products, the causes of failure, and planning new products), the academic world sees the development of new programs as an *innate* occurrence.

What Are the Basic Considerations in Developing New Programs?

The initiation of a new idea for an academic program has historically been the singular function of one or more interested faculty members. The decision to implement a new idea was a simple calculation based upon the size of an increased budget. Together, these factors accounted for a very streamlined system. But the complexity of today's environment, coupled with pressures for accountability and resources, have squeezed the free-spirit approach out of program development.

The planning process at most colleges and universities now includes a strategic approach that begins with a simultaneous look at external needs, opportunities, and constraints *and* internal strengths and capabilities. The assessment of external influences reveals what the institution *might do* or, sometimes, what it *should do*. Such an analysis proceeds with a series of questions: (1) What are the major trends in the environment? (2) What are the implications of these trends for the organization? and (3) What are the most significant opportunities and threats? (Kotler and Murphy 1981). Conversely, the assessment of the internal environment provides an indication of what the college or university can or cannot do. Systematic evaluations through such procedures as program reviews, accreditation exercises, or other means of self-assessment provide information on the quality of the institution's program resources. The next consideration has been described as the "matching" process (Shirley and Volkwein 1978). This process is one that entails matching external factors, internal strengths and capabilities, and mission. While different institutions place widely varied emphases on these considerations, the establishment of priorities for academic programs is the intended result.

Most of our time and effort in developing new programs are devoted to finding out whether the proposal for a program is viable. In the future, however, we need to begin to shift our emphasis to a more proactive consideration—not merely *whether* a proposed program is viable but *how* a new program will become successful.

To What Extent Have State and System Agencies Become Involved in Developing Academic Programs?

"Left totally to its own, the university will evolve toward self-interest rather than public interest" (Newman 1987, p. 70). Given such a pronouncement, it is not unreasonable to ask a question regarding state and system agencies' involvement in program development. Historically, the involvement of these agencies has been rather limited. Academic departments possess the competence to decide upon the structure and content of an academic program, while administrators make judgments about how the program relates to that particular institution's mission. It remains for the agencies to decide how a proposed new program relates to others in the state. Whether because of issues of accountability or fiscal constraint or program proliferation, the fact remains that state and system agencies have become much more involved in developing new programs. Most agencies have rewritten their policies for program approval within the last four years.

A number of trends have emerged. The process for approval has been considerably lengthened to include preproposal stages in most states and measures of postapproval performance in a number of states. The preproposal stage involves a preliminary iteration that formally announces an intention to plan. After reviewing the preproposal, institutions may then be given permission to submit an actual proposal for consideration. The concern for funding new programs has caused several states to begin asking specific questions regarding the reallocation of existing funds. Some attempt has been made to tie individual program proposals to statewide master planning or to require that institutions show how a proposed program fits within the campus's strategic planning. Multiple evaluative criteria have been enumerated to include such far-ranging topics as the characteristics of students, costs of accreditation, opportunities for employment, library holdings, projections for graduation, and five-year budgets. And finally, the scope of approving new programs has been greatly extended. Many state agencies now are responsible for also coordinating activities at technical and trade schools, community colleges, and private colleges and universities. In many instances, the definition of "new program" has been broadened to include majors and minors, concentrations, off-campus programs, and so on.

How Can the Process of Developing New Programs Be Improved?

The sources of ideas for new programs are too diffuse and the structure of colleges and universities too decentralized to adopt a generalized, lock-step set of management policies and procedures. The process is herky-jerky, with twists and turns throughout. Consequently, no "eight steps to success" or a universal "six-stage model" exists. There are, however, a number of practical prescriptions that do apply to developing new programs at most institutions:

1. *Create and maintain a climate for innovation of programs.* The leadership of an institution cannot neglect its responsibility for creating a climate that can overcome vested interests, shake up the status quo, fight territorialism, and generate resources to fuel innovative ideas. The climate for innovation begins with the leadership.
2. *Bring innovative people into the institution.* Because one of the most important characteristics of an innovative organization is its members' positive attitude toward

change, it is essential that innovators be actively recruited for available positions.

3. *Move innovative people around in the institution.* Complacency and comfortableness work to create stable personalities and social systems. And as stability increases, the rate of innovation decreases. The use of term appointments for some administrative positions and the effective recruiting of adjunct and visiting professors can bring a healthy dose of fresh air to a college or university.

4. *Guard against the trend toward increasing fragmentation.* As professors continue to be rewarded for specialization, the tendency is to translate those interests into the development of curricula. Given an environment in which new, specialized programs are added, few existing programs are discontinued, and resources are constrained, the result can be an institution that becomes dominated by far too many small, isolated, underfunded programs.

5. *Develop the means to look outward.* External constituencies can be an important source of new ideas and funds. They can also help to develop the specifics of a program by providing valuable feedback on proposals. By formalizing such "boundary-spanning" mechanisms as consortia of industry and faculty and advisory committees, the institution is in a better position to use external expertise in a process of continual revitalization.

6. *Separate the idea stage from the approval stage.* Innovation thrives on loners, change agents, informality, thinking out loud, brainstorming, and a decentralized organizational structure. The process of program approval, however, requires formalization, centralization, and the specific application of policies and procedures to operate efficiently. Innovators need to be protected from the frustrations of an extended bureaucratic approval process, and administrators in turn need to maintain their objectivity and prerogative to make decisions.

7. *Coordinate all activities related to program development through a limited number of persons or offices.* Depending upon the size of the institution, the responsibility for monitoring a proposed new program should remain with a single individual or a single office. Such an individual or office becomes the mechanism for negotiating the dis-

parities between faculty interests with administrative procedures that have become, at most institutions, a complicated and lengthy approval process.

8. *Integrate institutional research into all procedures for program development.* Both internal and external program approval processes have become so information intensive that the role of institutional research in managing academic data is crucial to effective and efficient development. Data gathering and analysis need to be included at the earliest possible stage of the process and continued through approval to evaluation.

9. *Visualize the development of new programs as a continuous, dynamic process.* Such evaluation activities as new program development, program review, and program discontinuance have been traditionally viewed as separate activities. A more appropriate perspective is to view the academic programs that an institution offers as its program portfolio. And as the institution's mission or environmental conditions change, that portfolio will necessarily evolve, with some new programs added, others reconfigured or strengthened, and still others discontinued.

10. *Develop a selective strategy.* Given the opportunity, every program can be justified as being *essential* to the mission of the institution. Accreditation agencies, program alumni, impassioned students, and tenured faculty can make for a strong advocacy group. Consequently, the desire and the means to make comparative judgments about proposed programs must both be available. Such judgments are part of a process that matches institutional strengths with a specifically defined mission—the result being a selective set of priorities.

11. *Integrate planning for academic programs with planning for finances and facilities.* New programs need to be given a chance to succeed. By not integrating financial and facilities planning, the administration takes the easy path of trying to make everyone happy. New programs are approved with no one willing to fight the battles. This live-and-let-live attitude can easily jeopardize the quality of the program, create a morale problem among students and faculty, and dampen further efforts at innovation.

12. *Coordinate internal and external processes for approval.*

The approval process for new programs has become increasingly complex. The process can be especially frustrating (and debilitating) if different questions are asked different ways for different purposes at different levels. Because state and system concerns are often different from campus concerns, such a possibility is a virtual certainty. The appropriate offices and individuals need to build a coordinated, comprehensive, and constructive approval process.

Developing new programs in most colleges and universities is merely adequate. It has been a product of faculty interests and a by-product of a growth environment. It has simply occurred. But such benign neglect will not be adequate in the future. Our thirst for information, changing social needs and technology, and an increasing demand for planning and accountability indicate the need for *innovation* in developing new academic programs.

ADVISORY BOARD

CONSULTING EDITORS

Charles Adams
Director, The Inquiry Program
Center for the Study of Adult and Higher Education
University of Massachusetts

Ann E. Austin
Research Assistant Professor
Vanderbilt University

Trudy W. Banta
Research Professor
University of Tennessee

Robert J. Barak
Deputy Executive Secretary
Director of Academic Affairs and Research
Iowa Board of Regents

Harriet W. Cabell
Associate Dean for Adult Education
Director, External Degree Program
University of Alabama

L. Leon Campbell
Provost and Vice President for Academic Affairs
University of Delaware

Ellen Earle Chaffee
Associate Commissioner for Academic Affairs
North Dakota State Board of Higher Education

Robert Paul Churchill
Chair and Associate Professor
Department of Philosophy
George Washington University

Peter T. Ewell
Senior Associate
National Center for Higher Education Management Systems

Reynolds Ferrante
Professor of Higher Education
George Washington University

Zelda F. Gamson
Director
New England Resource Center for Higher Education

J. Wade Gilley
Senior Vice President
George Mason University

Judy Diane Grace
Director of Research
Council for Advancement and Support of Education

Madeleine F. Green
Director, Center for Leadership Development
American Council on Education

Milton Greenberg
Provost
American University

Judith Dozier Hackman
Associate Dean
Yale University

Paul W. Hartman
Vice Chancellor for University Relations and Development
Texas Christian University

James C. Hearn
Associate Professor
University of Minnesota

Evelyn Hively
Vice President for Academic Programs
American Association of State Colleges and Universities

Frederic Jacobs
Dean of the Faculties
American University

Paul Jedamus
Professor
University of Colorado

Joseph Katz
Director, New Jersey Master Faculty Program
Woodrow Wilson National Fellowship Foundation

George Keller
Senior Vice President
The Barton-Gillet Company

L. Lee Knefelkamp
Dean, School of Education
American University

David A. Kolb
Professor and Chairman
Department of Organizational Behavior
The Weatherhead School of Management
Case Western Reserve University

Oscar T. Lenning
Vice President for Academic Affairs
Robert Wesleyan College

Charles J. McClain
President
Northeast Missouri State University

Judith B. McLaughlin
Research Associate on Education and Sociology
Harvard University

Marcia Mentkowski
Director of Research and Evaluation
Professor of Psychology
Alverno College

Richard I. Miller
Professor, Higher Education
Ohio University

James L. Morrison
Professor
University of North Carolina

Elizabeth M. Nuss
Executive Director
National Association of Student Personnel Administrators

Robert L. Payton
Director, Center on Philanthropy
Indiana University

Jack E. Rossmann
Professor of Psychology
Macalester College

Donald M. Sacken
Associate Professor
University of Arizona

Robert A. Scott
President
Ramapo College of New Jersey

CONTENTS

FOREWORD

Academic program change has been characterized by the following terms: slow, idiosyncratic, externally driven, ever present, and parochial. These aspects of program change are acceptable when: (1) the economy is stable and employment high, and rapid or massive program change is not crucial because there may not be a perceived need for change; (2) society's expectations for higher education are low, as before World War II when college graduates made up a low percentage of the total workforce; (3) the knowledge base is stable, and the content of the program is unchanging; and (4) higher education is growing significantly and can nurture change without threatening established programs, as in the 1960s when institutions could easily change their academic programs by simply adding new faculty and new program directions.

Most of the conditions that support this slow and evolutionary process of change do not exist today. Most notably, the dynamics in the world economy has contributed to increased public dissatisfaction with college outcomes. Growth in enrollments for institutions of higher education has slowed, and therefore institutions are not routinely expanding their curricula. This lack of growth has contributed to a stagnation within the faculty. The viability of an aging conservative faculty is compounded by rapid developments in new teaching technologies, as well as significant increases in the growth of the knowledge base in many scientific areas.

There is a consensus developing that colleges can no longer tolerate being dependent upon program change brought on by individual inspiration or idiosyncratic evolution. Institutions need to be concerned about their organizational structure, leadership, and procedures to ensure that effective program change will occur.

This report, written by Daniel Seymour, currently a visiting scholar at the Higher Education Research Institute at UCLA, offers a systematic framework for examining the issue of academic program change by concentrating on the overlapping of three areas: organizational innovation, strategic planning, and program evaluation. Seymour identifies twelve specific practical prescriptions that colleges and universities can use to enhance the climate of their institutions for developing, promoting, sustaining, and refining academic programs.

The effect of external conditions on higher education institutions and the need for program change has been well-documented by many national reports. The ability to respond, to change, and to adapt may be the distinguishing trait between those institutions that continue to prosper, and those that don't.

Jonathan D. Fife
Professor and Director
ERIC Clearinghouse on Higher Education
School of Education and Human Development
The George Washington University

ACKNOWLEDGMENTS

I am particularly grateful for the support and sound advice of Christopher Rigaux, the managing editor of the ASHE-ERIC series, and four scrutinous yet softly spoken reviewers. "I thank you for your voices. Thank you" (Shakespeare, *Coriolanus,* act 2, scene 3, line 179).

ORGANIZATIONS AND INNOVATION

From Social Change to Individual Creativity

Nothing stays the same. People, organizations, and societies are in a continual state of metamorphosis. The inevitability of the process, however, does not mean that the nature and scope of the alteration cannot be controlled. Social change, for example, has been defined as the "alteration in the structure and function of a social system" (Zaltman and Duncan 1977, p. 8). While such a definition appears to view change as a somewhat fortuitous event, other social scientists have taken care to note that change is any unplanned *or planned* alteration in the status quo (e.g., Lippitt et al. 1973, p. 37). As uneventful as this addendum may sound, the history of "planned change" is a rather provocative one.

The idea of social scientists' participating in and actively influencing social change has been a point of controversy in America since the notion developed in the late 19th century, and an ideological question has been the center of this controversy: Should people seek, through deliberative forethought, to mold the shape of their collective future, or should confidence be placed in a principle of automatic adjustment? The "planners" have seen an important role for social science in creating policy initiatives that attempt to manage human affairs—and destinies. In contrast, "automatic adjusters" have tended to relegate social scientists to the role of passive observers and to deny them participation in influencing the direction or form of social practices. In many respects, social upheavals like the Great Depression, World Wars I and II, and the Vietnam conflict have strengthened the resolve of social planners. In fact, it has been observed, since the 1950s most people in our society have come to believe that we must seek to influence the future patterns of our lives, to plan social changes (Benne, Chin, and Bennis 1985, p. 16).

When we refer to change on a societal level, we are usually concerned with the dynamics of the change process. The nature of the transformation is studied in terms of such process variables as alienation, power, and turbulence. When our level of analysis shifts to the study of orderly systems, that is, organizations within a society, the notion of change is usually replaced by the concept of innovation. Change and innovation are not the same thing. An innovation is an idea, practice, or material artifact that is perceived as *new* by the relevant unit of adoption (Zaltman and Duncan 1977, p. 12). The innovation may be a distinctive technology incorporated into a new consumer prod-

Most people in our society have come to believe that we must seek to influence the future patterns of our lives, to plan social changes.

uct, it may be a new organizational structure, perhaps in a service firm, or it may be a new instructional method introduced into the educational system. The innovation is the change object, and as such it is a tool to exploit change. But whereas all innovations imply change, not all change involves innovation, because not every modification is perceived as one of a kind.

Finally, the changes in society that are driven by organizational innovations are propelled by the creative energies of individuals. Creativity, like planned social change, has a stormy past. Creativity is freedom, an unencumbered ability to choose. But the notion forwarded by the 18th century philosopher Rousseau that "man is born free" had the odor of blasphemy (Bloom 1987, p. 180). God alone had been called the Creator, and the thought that man could create and choose without "guidance from nature" was a denial of the supremacy of God. A modern-day social scientist, however, sees individuals as being able to control their earthly destiny. This control manifests itself in the form of active problem solving. Individuals sense an incompleteness or disharmony, and the resulting tensions that are aroused are not satisfied by routine responses— old answers are not adequate. Solutions are tested by rearranging or manipulating and a new order of things is sought. This way of thinking about creativity has been described as:

> . . . the process of becoming sensitive to problems, deficiencies, gaps in knowledge, missing elements, disharmonies, and so on; identifying the difficulty; searching for solutions; making guesses or formulating hypotheses about the deficiencies; testing and retesting them; and finally communicating the results (Torrance 1965, p. 665).

This herky-jerky process of discovery is the individual's source of self-renewal, relief, and liberation.

The literature that has emerged on organizational innovation can be divided into four categories. While the headings (categories) used for the remainder of this section are not totally exhaustive—and certainly not mutually exclusive—they do provide a decision-oriented framework. For example, the first category of research and writings is concerned with the *process* of innovation. "To innovate," the verb, is the process of creating new ways of doing things—from the tension of individual creativity to implementation or acceptance. Do certain institutional characteristics of colleges and universities impede the process of innovation? Can administrators control the environment in such a way as to minimize the effects?

A second category of literature targets the *people* of innovation. People, through individual creativity, are responsible for the act of innovation, and it is people who eventually adopt or reject it. Can characteristics of innovators be identified in higher education? Do specific mechanisms include such innovators in decision processes? The third category is the *product* of innovation. "Innovation," the noun, describes the object—for example, ideas, practices, products, or new academic programs developed in higher education. Is it possible to identify characteristics of products that are related to successful innovation? Can colleges and universities manage the attributes of program innovation? And the last category of literature details organizational *strategies* to facilitate successful innovation.

Innovation—The Process
Environmental factors explain many aspects of individual, social, and organizational change. Certainly social change is fueled by reaction to a disruptive and capricious environment. The innovative programs of Franklin Roosevelt's New Deal, for instance, were the direct consequence of the Great Depression. President Kennedy's shift of priorities and resources to a national space program in the early 1960s was precipitated by a Russian cosmonaut's pioneering space flight. It has even been observed that "so stubborn are the defenses of a mature society against change that shock treatment is often required to bring about renewal. A nation will postpone critically important social changes until war or depression forces the issue" (Gardner 1964, p. 44). Organizations are equally as reactive. Extraorganizational forces may in fact be the most significant variable in explaining innovative behavior. The corporate organization, for example, is more likely to innovate when its environment is rapidly changing than when it is steady. Such factors as market conditions, technological change, the needs and demands of clientele, and the labor market have been shown to be major determinants of innovation (Burns and Stalker 1961). This reactive mode is not a phenomenon peculiar only to the competition-driven world of the modern corporation, and "most innovations in public-service institutions are imposed on them either by outsiders or by catastrophe" (Drucker 1985, p. 177).

A second generalization regarding the process of innovation

follows quite logically from the notion of "external threat." Each disturbance results in a natural tendency to return to a period of calm—even complacency. This phenomenon, commonly referred to as "homeostasis," is usually exemplified by the tendency of the human body to use regulatory mechanisms to maintain constancy in such physiological states as temperature or blood sugar. Exercise increases pulse rate, but "resistance" to this change presently brings the heartbeat back to a state of equilibrium. Individuals, organizations, and societies exhibit internal processes that counteract any departure from the normal. It has been suggested that the reluctance to admit having weaknesses, awkwardness and fear of failure associated with doing something different, bad experiences with past efforts at change, and concern about the possible loss of present satisfaction are the general factors that may account for homeostasis (Lippitt, Watson, and Wesley 1958, pp. 180–81).

A number of general theories focus on the process of innovation in organizations. Each takes a different perspective based upon a different set of assumptions. One approach sees organizational innovation as being a function of the cognitive limitations of problem solvers (March and Simon 1958), while another is structured around the manner in which organizations deal with stable and changing environments (Burns and Stalker 1961). A third perspective emphasizes the relationship between incentive systems and organizational conflict (Wilson 1966); another focuses on patterns of organizational adaptation (Harvey and Mills 1970). Finally, several organizational researchers concentrate on the specification of organizational characteristics affecting the initiation of innovation (the generation and development of a novel idea or approach) and its implementation (the actual use of the innovation by the organization's members) (Hage and Aiken 1970; Zaltman, Duncan, and Holbek 1973).

The bulk of the empirical research and case studies on organizations has focused on the intraorganizational characteristics that impede the process of innovation. The following literature is organized by topics that have been investigated across many different types of organizational structures—hospitals, community and charitable organizations, large corporations and small businesses, among others. While not an exhaustive review, the topics are some of the more consistent and interesting results related to organizational innovation. The initial set of organizational issues is cultural; that is, they relate to the system of norms, beliefs and assumptions, and values that determine how people in the organization act. The second set is structural in orientation, relating to the characteristics of the organizational framework.

Cultural impediments

"Cultural" in this instance is viewed as a general, holistic concept that includes social and psychological influences. This impediment is particularly important because it is an internal counterbalance to an environmental threat. Few psychological traits of human beings in organizations are so universal as that of suspicion and hostility toward outside influences (Watson 1972, p. 616). The basic response to change initiated outside the organization is to first discredit and then to discard. Outside ideas are often perceived as not being relevant to "our way of doing things." Another response is "It's fine, but it wouldn't work in our system." Even outside *opportunities* can be discredited. The impact is a type of cultural ethnocentrism that can make resistance to change endemic in organizations. For example, of 58 major innovations that occurred within the last 100 years, the established or then-dominant firm in 56 cases failed to make the necessary transition:

- Gas utilities failed to capitalize on the emerging electrical utility business.
- Manufacturers of mechanical calculators watched from the sidelines as electronic calculators swept the market.
- Vacuum tube manufacturers refused to enter the transistor business, concentrating instead on making better vacuum tubes (Little 1984, p. 60).

"Vested interests" are another problem confronting the organization in its attempts to innovate. In any organization, many of the established ways of doing things are held in place not by logic or even by ritual but by the fact that any change could jeopardize the rights, privileges, or advantages of specific individuals. As people in organizations develop vested interests, the organization itself becomes more inflexible—it rigidifies. This calcification extends beyond the level of the single individual to include an organizational "sunk cost mentality." A discussion of the mature product trap notes that successful mature businesses have a major stake in maintaining their existing business (Little 1984, p. 61). They have large investments

in terms of production facilities, technologies, and market position in their product areas. When a new threat or opportunity occurs, the reaction of the established firm often is, "We've got so much invested or sunk in the old business—we can't change now!"

A slightly more formalized impediment is power—or more specifically, the lack of power. The power-equalization concept has been frequently invoked to account for organizational resistance to implementing innovations (Leavitt 1965). This explanation assumes that members of an organization who must adopt or concur with an innovation will resist it unless they have been involved in formulating the innovation in the first place. This phenomenon has been consistently documented in different research settings. For example, a study of 115 scientists, each of whom had been the director of a research project, found "influence over decision making" was related to "innovativeness" (Andrews 1975). Those individuals who felt they had less influence also were less inclined to be associated with innovative ideas.

The process of developing a new product in business is often spearheaded by a product champion—someone who negotiates the bureaucratic maze and leads the fight to have a new concept considered. Such individuals are often "loners," isolated from their discipline and on the periphery of organizational happenings, but they are also considered to be important to the process of innovation. Another impediment to innovation is that such pioneering individuals are up against continual pressure to conform to norms. Members of the organization demand that the habits of the individual correspond to those of the group, the behavior described in Whyte's classic study, *The Organization Man* (1956). The behavior includes time schedules, modes of dress, indications of loyalty to the company, personal ambition to rise, and appropriate forms of consumption. While norms provide stability and behavioral guidelines that define what individuals can expect from one another (and consequently are essential for the conduct of any social system), they are also strong disincentives for individuals (or change agents) to engage in innovative behavior (Zaltman and Duncan 1977, p. 74).

A final, and perhaps most apparent, cultural force that impedes innovation in organizations is the climate, that is, the degree to which individuals in the organization do not support change. At least three important dimensions of climate for change can be identified (Duncan 1972). The *need for change* focuses on the perception that individuals have about the need for change in the organization. The *openness to change* is concerned with the perception that individuals have concerning the willingness of others to support change. And the *potential for change* deals with the perception that individuals have about the ability of the organization to implement change. In fact, one longitudinal study of program changes in social welfare organizations found that various measures of "attitude toward change" were associated with the rate of program change (Hage and Aiken 1967). Such personality variables of the personnel are strong predictors of innovation. "It could be argued that change occurs in organizations because the organization has a high proportion of individuals who are favorably oriented to social change" (p. 513). Without this obvious predisposition, change comes slowly, if at all.

In summary, the evidence regarding those cultural forces that have a negative impact on innovation is quite straightforward: *All of the forces that contribute to stability in personality or in social systems influence the rate of innovation.* The greater the stability, the less innovation that occurs. Resistance is endemic in organizations:

> *Enduring systems are overdetermined in that they have more than one mechanism to product stability. For example, they select personnel to meet role requirements, train them to fill specific roles, and socialize them with sanctions and rewards to carry out prescribed patterns. Thus, when it comes to change, organizations show defenses in depth* (Katz and Kahn 1978, p. 714).

Structural impediments

While many more studies and writings deal with structure than culture, the conclusions are far more tenuous when it comes to structural effects on innovation. Take, for example, the question of an organization's size; the conclusions are diverse:

> *Size has a strong positive effect on innovation which supports other research (e.g., Baldridge and Burnham 1975) that also shows that large organizations have decisive advantages over small ones in their capacity to innovate* (Blau and McKinley 1979, p. 210).

The larger the organization, the higher the probability that its collective decision processes will focus on short-run, internal problems and select minimally dissatisficing solutions to the[m] rather than focusing upon external, long-run opportunities or those aspects of the alternatives that relate to their consequences (Steffire 1985, p. 7).

Perhaps size per se is not the explanatory variable (Mohr 1969). Instead, the key may be the added resources that can accompany larger organizations. So while a larger organization may have more constrained decision processes, the additional resources that are available can be enough to compensate. The problem for organizations is that they find it easy to grow; in fact, getting bigger is almost a universally recognized measure of success. And while they gain various economies of scale in the process, they lose the advantages that characterize many smaller organizations—flexibility, adaptability, and simplicity.

Several other structural characteristics of organizations have been tested. Complexity, defined as the number of occupational specialties in the organization (Hage and Aiken 1970, p. 33), has been the subject of numerous studies, with somewhat conflicting results. For example, while increased complexity could lead to increased innovation (Baldridge and Burnham 1975, p. 170), others conclude that "these results indicate that structural complexity impedes innovation" (Blau and McKinley 1979, p. 210). One explanation for these contradictory conclusions is that the complexity of the organization can have both positive and negative effects on various stages of innovation (Zaltman, Duncan, and Holbek 1973, p. 137). At initiation, individuals in highly diverse organizations (e.g., a college or university) have more opportunity to discover and pursue areas for innovation. At implementation, however, high complexity can impede innovation because it may be extremely difficult for any single source of authority to give priority to one proposal over another. The resulting conflict is often a devisive and unproductive power struggle for attention.

Another structural characteristic, formalization, has also received considerable attention in the study of organizations. Formalization is the emphasis placed within the organization on following specific rules and procedures in performing one's job (Zaltman, Duncan, and Holbek 1973, p. 138). Again, the results of various studies appear to differ along the lines of initiation versus implementation. Numerous studies (e.g., Hage and

Aiken 1967; Kahn et al. 1964) have found a strong negative relationship between measures of formalization and the rate of innovation. But it has also been concluded that "it is not possible, on the basis of the data, to draw the conclusion that formalized organizations and formal control instruments guiding the process are always detrimental to innovativeness" (Normann 1971, p. 215). The explanation is that high formalization impedes innovation at initiation when rules and procedures act as restraints. In contrast, when concerned with the implementation of innovation, specific formalized procedures may reduce resistance (Shepard 1967). As with the topic of complexity, these results also have obvious implications for higher education organizations.

Finally, centralization is conceptualized in terms of the locus of the authority and decision making in the organization (Zaltman, Duncan, and Holbek 1973, p. 143). The greater the hierarchy of authority (centralization of decision making in the upper ranks), the lesser the rate of innovation. Centralization affects innovation by restricting the channels of communication; information flow and commitment are reduced. And in a centralized organization, it is simply easier for the innovation to be vetoed (Thompson 1969)—or if not vetoed, then simply rearranged or reconstituted in the process. One study of failures of new products (Crawford 1979) found that the dominant reason for failure was that the product had no real competitive advantage—at least from customers' point of view. The organizational problem in the study was that product development tended to produce products that exhibited characteristics that fit the internal line of resistance rather than the market demand. Thus, it follows that of the major organizational decision-making models defined as collegial, bureaucratic, political, rational, and anarchical, the bureaucratic model produces the least amount of change (Chaffee 1983, p. 22). It should also be noted, however, that the effects of centralization can vary. The initiation of innovation thrives on decentralized decision making. Information is more readily available, and commitment and ownership are increased. With the implementation of innovation, however, more strict lines of authority can help reduce potential conflict and ambiguity.

The literature on higher education has progressed in much the same manner as the more general literature on organizations. Some writings have concentrated on analyzing colleges and universities as evolving institutions and approach their

---

work descriptively. Such an approach is generally passive in nature and merely attempts to document the forces and effects of change. The Carnegie Commission on Higher Education's study (Hodgkinson 1971), for example, describes many changes in institutional characteristics, including demographics of the student body and degrees awarded. Other authors (e.g., Christenson 1982) have reviewed the environmental forces and impacts that create changes in higher education. Some major efforts have been prescriptive in nature, offering strategies for planned change: the use of campus change teams to renew higher education from within (Sikes, Schlesinger, and Seashore 1974), the description of patterns of change that characterize various types of academic innovations (Martorana and Kuhns 1975), the synthesis of a series of characteristics of innovation associated with successful innovations (Levine 1980), the development of a model based upon five factors critical to introducing change into a university (Lindquist 1978), and the use of both case study materials and survey research data to study the process of academic reform (Hefferlin 1969).

In general, the literature on higher education has progressed from the study of change to the study of planned change to specific efforts to understand and implement innovative practices and procedures. Much of this literature has been described in *The Process of Change in Higher Education Institutions* (Nordvall 1982), which offers several broad guidelines regarding the process of change:

- In a college or university, change cannot be ordered by top administrators.
- A prime way that an institution explores the need to change is through a program of institutional research.
- It is very difficult to institute change in an institution where little perceived need for change exists.
- Even if the advice about instituting change is followed, an effort to establish change can still fail (pp. 42–43).

Most of the focused research and writings on the process of innovation in higher education have been limited to two areas—structure and decision making. Colleges and universities are organized internally upon the principle of a community of authority. Each major subgroup—students, faculty, administration, and alumni—divides into numerous smaller units, each with its own goals, norms, campus location, group identity, and pattern of interaction (Lindquist 1974, p. 325). Within the faculty community, the institution is further divided by general field (e.g., oceanography) and specific discipline (e.g., chemical oceanography), each with its own way of approaching intellectual questions. The effect is to further isolate individuals from any hierarchy of authority. Policies such as academic freedom and tenure and procedures such as the various review committees within colleges and faculty governing bodies all contribute to a diffusion of power, and "academic institutions are deliberately structured to resist precipitant change" (Hefferlin 1969, p. 16). This type of organizational structure has been described as a "loosely coupled system" (Weick 1976). The dominant example of this loose coupling is the interdependence between members of one department and another, say, for example, between the economics department and the marketing department. While members of these two units may serve in a faculty senate together, do research in an area of mutual interest, even team teach a course, they preserve their own identity and physical separateness. Their relationship is impermanent and dissolvable.

The structural organization of college faculties into disciplines has evolved to the point that "the department" is the basic organizational unit of most colleges and universities. The "potent force" that has become the department is evident in the following description of the problems relating to an expanded program review process at the University of Kansas:

A . . . problem . . . has to do with departments who unilaterally decide that they are "too busy" to enter into the program review process, or that they have too many problems at the moment to undergo review, [or] that a concurrent accreditation is taking too much of their time, or the like. Several departments in [the] university have in effect refused to cooperate in the review process. In the face of their collective stubbornness, the process has broken down. What can be done about that problem is unclear. When an academic department refuses to admit the review committee and announces its intention to subvert the process, the response tends to be one of bafflement and confusion. The resolution of this recalcitrance awaits a more ingenious mind (Lincoln 1986, p. 21).

As the core of a decentralized, informalized, complex organiza-

Literature on higher education has progressed from the study of change to the study of planned change to specific efforts to understand and implement innovative practices and procedures.

tion, the departmental unit has tremendous *potential* to initiate innovation. Some research, however, has shown that being a smaller, independent unit does not by itself ensure innovation. One study of curriculum change, for example, found that under conditions of adversity, departments with strong reputations were not likely to engage in modifying the curriculum (Manns and March 1978). Further, increasing specialization does not take advantage of the fact that many innovations occur on the boundaries of disciplines. Departmentalization also tends to distribute the change-oriented faculty so they cannot develop a critical mass (Sikes, Schlesinger, and Seashore 1974, p. 40). One vice president for academic affairs even went so far as to say recently, "Department structure seriously conflicts with the basic mission of higher education institutions. Many administrators and faculty members are reluctant to address this problem for fear they will disturb the peace. The status quo appear to be too solid . . . " (Rawlings 1987, p. B2). Finally, one of the major difficulties inherent in such an organizational structure involves the links between the various structures. Academic systems can be divided into operating units (the understructure), the college or university in its entirety (the middle-structure), and the links that relate the one enterprise to the other (the superstructure), and "the three levels often march to different drummers, having different directions, sources, and vehicles of change" (Clark 1983, p. 105).

In contrast to structure, a second area of interest regarding the process of innovation has focused on decision making in higher education. Five organizational models of decision making in higher education have been described in the literature: the bureaucratic model, the collegial model, the rational model, the political model, and the organized anarchy model (Chaffee 1983; Ellstrom 1983; Havelock 1973). While all of these models have received attention in the literature, especially "organized anarchies" and "garbage cans" (Cohen and March 1974), the political model has been the one most studied in terms of innovation. In the competition for scarce resources, some students of decision theory contend that all decisions made by a university are political, incapable of rational decisions. Since the seminal work, *Power and Conflict in the University* (Baldridge 1971), a number of researchers have applied the concept of power and conflict to the study of innovation. Political links in the process of academic innovation have led to the suggestion of seven characteristics that form political obstacles to innovation:

1. Most change of any magnitude, especially in times of scarce resources, threatens secured positions.
2. Extreme differentiation and fragmentation are apparent within institutions of higher education.
3. The power to implement academic decisions tends to be pluralistic rather than monolithic.
4. The "academic revolution" presents firm value resistance to innovations that challenge meritocracy, specialization, and experience-based beliefs.
5. Educational outcomes and future demands on the institution are inadequately measured.
6. Most college and university members are isolated from new information about teaching and learning.
7. University structures and functions are intended to carry out established practices by established means (Lindquist 1974, p. 325).

The use of political power in the allocation of resources has specific application to processes of innovation and has received considerable attention (Hackman 1985; Rutherford, Fleming, and Mathias 1985; Salancik and Pfeffer 1974).

Finally, several different authors offer extremely useful "lists" related to the process of innovation. Zaltman and Duncan (1977, pp. 379–94), for example, distill a comprehensive set of principles of planned change that can serve as general guidelines for successful innovation. Of particular interest for higher education is the section on strategies to effect change. While many of the principles may seem obvious—for example, "It is important for the organization to scan its environment, . . . a critical source of ideas for change and innovation" (p. 391)—it is just such obvious principles that are often ignored or forgotten in the development of new academic programs.

More specific to higher education are some rules for building effective political support in the process of innovation (Baldridge 1980, pp. 126–27) and an organization of the work of numerous authors into 12 discrete categories of prescriptions for planned change in colleges and universities (Levine 1980, pp. 210–11). Baldridge's list is based upon case studies of innovative processes at over 40 colleges and universities, and the rules are useful because they have emerged from an analysis of a single innovation that was funded by the Exxon Education Foundation and awarded to a diverse group of institutions. The rules are limited to practical strategies with broad implications, for example, "Concentrate your efforts. People interested in changing the system frequently squander their efforts by chasing too many rainbows. An effective political change agent concentrates on only the important issues" (p. 126). Levine's synthesis of "planned change" theories, while not going into full detail, provides a useful set of highlights or guideposts specific to colleges and universities. For example, the category "build a base of active support" includes "involve those who are affected," "build coalitions," "aim for personal commitment to change among participants," and "encourage ownership."

While some disagreement exists regarding the nature and impact of specific structural elements on innovation, little doubt remains that organizational structures in general evolve to protect the interests of the current set of occupants. In that regard, the organizations within higher education are no different. Many innovations, including those generated within the campus walls, fail because they are unable to negotiate existing structural constraints.

Innovation—The People

While it has been shown that the process of innovation is a function of the structure and culture of the organization, it has also been noted that the prime explanatory factor regarding innovation is the attitudes of people—"Is change needed?" "Am I going to benefit?" It is the individual, then, that plays a key role in whether innovation is initiated and implemented within an organization, and one way to look at innovation is to distinguish between two groups of people—the target of change and the agent of change (Zaltman and Duncan 1977).

The most substantial research regarding the targets of change was conducted more than 25 years ago (Rogers 1962). That synthesis of over 500 publications classifies individuals within a social system on the basis of innovativeness. The premise is that because all individuals do not adopt an innovation at the same time, a classification along a time continuum would result in "categories of adopters." The resulting categorization system delineates five types of adopters and the proportion of the population that fits into each category: innovators (2.5 percent), early adopters (13.5 percent), early majority (34 percent), late majority (34 percent), and laggards (16 percent). Evidence presented supports the discrimination of these categories based upon personal characteristics, social status, financial position, mental ability, communication behavior, and social relationships. While a number of alternative innovation adoption models have been proposed (e.g., Howard and Sheth 1969; Robertson 1971) and numerous tests and applications performed, the basic thrust of the research is the confirmation of an epidemic model (i.e., spreading through a social system in some identifiable and predictable manner) of adoption of innovation. The current use of this approach is with the introduction and marketing of new products to commercial markets, but much of the original application was in the study of the diffusion of new ideas in rural sociology and education (Ross 1958).

The other actors in the process of innovation are commonly referred to as "change agents." Agents of change may be internal or external to the organization, but their mission remains the same—to initiate and implement a change from the status quo. The importance of such people to an organization cannot be underestimated. In fact, one study of innovation in organizations concludes that "innovation does not require free resources so much as it requires people to push innovation" (Daft and Becker 1978, p. 154). Again, most research and writing in this area concentrate on the identification of characteristics of successful change agents (Havelock and Havelock 1973), which include the three general topic areas of attitudes and values, knowledge, and skills. Other major efforts include the development of a number of generalizations concerning success of change agents based upon an extensive review of the literature about change (Rogers and Shoemaker 1971) and the enumeration of a detailed list of desirable qualifications of change agents, including technical qualifications, administrative ability, leadership skills, and political finesse (Zaltman and Duncan 1977).

Within higher education, a few isolated studies have examined agents and targets of change. Evans (1982) and Evans and Leppmann (1968), for example, studied the problem of resistance to instructional technology in higher education and applied Rogers's "adopter categories" to college professors. Evans found that innovators come generally from the more pragmatic areas of the university and that they are removed from the academic endeavors of the university, particularly classroom teaching. He also found that:

- To become an innovator, one needs a cosmopolite orientation, that is, one external to a particular system.
- The laggard has a localite orientation, his or her horizon is limited, and his or her information sources are found within a narrowly defined environment.
- The extreme laggard could be described as an isolate or at least a semi-isolate (p. 94).

In a broader sense, "the faculty" has been identified as the primary barrier to change because of inertia caused by disciplinary orientation, internal divisions, and a process that accords them veto power (Levine 1978, p. 425). Another explanation is the simple lack of motivation: "Faculty frequently express an obligation and the competence to participate but put low priority on actual participation" (Floyd 1985, p. 63).

Leadership and administrators' styles of leadership relative to innovation have also received some attention—although a modest amount. In fact, the literature on this topic "leaves a good deal to be desired" (Gushkin and Bassis 1985, p. 16). The most dominant styles of leadership in higher education do not facilitate the most creative innovational climates (Gushkin and Bassis 1985). One style, however, although not common in higher education, is the most effective in facilitating innovation: The "team leader" style places the primary emphasis on creating an interpersonal environment among senior administrators where mutual respect, a strong delegation of authority, and a great deal of mutual influence exist (Gushkin and Bassis 1985). This style emphasizes the use of that influence and attempts to deemphasize the exercise of authority. It also concentrates on the process by which decisions are made rather than the decisions themselves. A series of case studies on entrepreneurship and the college presidency (of small colleges) identifies several characteristics of successful presidential change agents (Peck 1983, 1984, 1985). First, an entrepreneurial president has an exaggerated sense of mission. Second, he or she also expects opportunities to exist by paying attention to changes in the environment. Third, their most important decisions about the future are intuitive. Fourth, they improve their intuitions by using a comprehensive intelligence-gathering net-

work. Fifth, these presidents take risks and, sixth, they innovate; they are always doing new things, doing old things new
ways, doing things differently, assuming a new attitude, or
adopting a new perspective. Others have examined the propens-
ity for risk among academic administrators (Jellema 1986;
Seymour 1987). Seymour's study of college and university administrators and business executives based on a large sample
found that administrators and executives who had been in
upper-level management for under five years were not significantly different in terms of risk taking. When the more experi-
enced administrators (over 10 years) were compared to
executives, however, the academics emerged as significantly
more adverse to risks. Several aspects of the academic environment tend to infringe on the innovative spirit of administrators:

- A high percentage of administrators who are sole products
  of academe;
- An inability to implement strategies that optimize the efficiency of the university;
- A fragmented staff that has few common goals;
- A large group of constituents with opposing viewpoints
  and objectives;
- A reward system that values inaction in situations involving choices where certainty is not guaranteed;
- A belief that change is the mandate of the faculty, not the
  administration (p. 37).

In addition to the president, one other college administrator
has been targeted in the literature as an agent of change. Given
that the complexities of the change process require on-campus
professional support to coordinate and expedite the process, any
planned change model should rely heavily on an institutional
researcher (Winstead 1982). An even more pronounced role of
change agent suggests that the job of an institutional researcher
is to carry out studies that "force administrators and faculty
members to reexamine their goals as well as their practices"
(p. 310). One recent article advocates that institutional researchers become change agents—skillful catalysts and facilita-
tors of data-based decisions and follow-through—and recom-
mends that greater attention be given to skills involving people and the change process in institutional research literature
and that training programs be developed and implemented to
teach those skills (Terrass and Pomrenke 1981).

A number of comprehensive lists have been developed that are useful to academicians—a series of knowledge and skill areas (Fessler 1976, pp. 32–35), a complete list of tactics for change agents for implementation (Martorana and Kuhns 1975, pp. 167–72), and an exhaustive set of characteristics of successful change agents (Havelock and Havelock 1973, pp. 70–72). Of particular interest is Winstead's enumeration of the characteristics, functions, and activities of the specialist in planned changes in higher education:

- An internal catalyst for change
- A sensitivity to the changing demands in higher education
- The identification of promising alternatives to current practices
- A resource to those responsible for clarifying institutional goals
- The monitoring of progress toward institutional goals
- An assistant in deriving measurable objectives for the institution
- A mediator in various conflicts
- A "question asker" and an "idea stimulator"
- A disseminator of internal innovations
- A creator of appropriate institutional renewal processes (Winstead 1982, pp. 26–27).

Winstead then uses these functions, activities, and characteristics to drive a broad-based change model—one that involves a systematic planning process.

The most obvious conclusion one can make about this literature is that it reinforces the image of a college or university as a fragmented, divisive organization. "The final ingredient that is required for a creative university environment consists of integrating mechanisms that serve to stimulate communication and experimentation" (Gushkin and Bassis 1985, p. 18). The use of multiunit teams, task forces, and project centers should encourage the exchange of ideas and information across organizational boundaries to help break down the isolation and orientation toward special interests that is prevalent in higher education institutions. This "integrating mechanisms theme" is similar to the adaptive means included in the "integrating structures theme" inherent in Clark's discussion of an academic superstructure—links that relate the operating units to the administrative structure.

Innovation—The Product

Another rubric in the literature on innovation focuses on the innovation itself. The "product" can be an idea, a process, an organizational structure, a service, or a tangible product. Again, Rogers spearheaded much of the formative research in this area (1962), identifying five different generalizable characteristics of successful innovations. The first characteristic is *relative advantage*, or the degree to which an innovation is superior to the ideas it supersedes. The more that an individual or group perceives that a product has a distinct advantage, the greater the likelihood that it will be adopted. *Compatibility*, the second characteristic, is the degree to which an innovation is consistent with existing values and past experiences of the adopters. Compatibility is also a matter of perception. The greater the perceived compatibility, the greater the likelihood of adoption. The third characteristic is *complexity*—the degree to which an innovation is relatively difficult to understand and use. Along a complexity/simplicity continuum, the greater the perceived simplicity of an innovation, the greater the likelihood of adoption. *Divisibility*, the fourth characteristic, is defined as the degree to which an innovation may be tried on a limited basis. The divisibility of an innovation, as perceived by members of a social system, affects its rate of adoption. Small-scale trials increase the likelihood of adoption. Finally, *communicability* is the degree to which the results of an innovation can be easily observed and described. If the perceived communicability is low, the likelihood of adoption will also be low. Understandably, most of the application of Rogers's typology has been with consumer and industrial products, although it has been shown to be applicable to nonprofit organizations (Kotler 1982), including higher education (Levine 1980, p. 184).

Within higher education, the interest in innovation, the product, has ranged from organizational changes to the adoption of new technologies to the development of new programs. For example, one recurrent theme has been the reorganization of liberal arts colleges and liberal education to reflect societal changes. The situation calls for "an innovative spirit" and an overt "appeal for innovation" (Henderson 1970; Martin 1969). More recently, another question has been asked: "What conditions are necessary to support and nurture the growth of innovations when they are introduced into colleges and universities?" (Baldridge 1980, p. 117). The research in this particular case focused on 49 institutions that had received Resource Allocation and Management Program (RAMP) awards from the Exxon Education Foundation. The innovation was managerial; the study discovered the patterns of behavior that supported efforts at managerial improvement and, in contrast, the behavior that undercut those improvements. Among other conclusions, it noted that managerial innovations require "top administration support" and "a security blanket to minimize vulnerability" and that "staff turnover kills a project" (pp. 131–33).

Instructional innovation has received considerable attention. An analysis of the innovative practices related to instructional technology using a cross-sectional survey and focused interview data from administrators and professors at 10 universities produced several guidelines:

1. *Meaningful long-range planning must be a vital part of any attempt to introduce innovations within the institution.*
2. *Carefully preplanned reinforcement schedules for those willing to contribute to the adoption of the innovation, projected over a long . . . period, will assist in the institutionalization of the innovation.*
3. *It will become necessary to determine the most effective type of reinforcement to assure continuation of the innovation. In some instances, salary increments are used. Other incentives include public acknowledgment and appreciation for those involved with the innovation.*
4. *Unless long-range institutional support and commitment are evident, innovations of any type are likely to be short-lived* (Evans 1982, p. 101).

In a similar manner, another recent study reviewed the use of a multimedia, self-instructional learning module (SLATE) among 21 faculty members at Michigan State University (Davis et al. 1982). Four factors emerged as important to successful innovation (1) how fully the innovators were supported by their departments; (2) the ease with which their SLATE was introduced into the curriculum; (3) the extent to which their SLATE incorporated features that were necessary for its success; and (4) the level of their motivation.

Finally, a number of studies have examined specific programs. The New Directions for Higher Education series has two sourcebooks on program development, one in graduate programs and the other in career programs in a liberal arts context. The first, *Keeping Graduate Programs Responsive to National Needs* (Pelczar and Solman 1984), has individual chapters on such topics as organizational and procedural impediments, the use of cost-benefit analysis to encourage innovation, assessing the quality of innovative programs, and links between the university and industry, and explores new program trends in music, philosophy, history, literature, education, and engineering. This volume is important because it is the result of the merging of two perspectives: the desire to document the development of new graduate programs in institutions across the country and an interest in trying to understand how universities have adapted their offerings to the new needs of the labor market. In the second, *Creating Career Programs in a Liberal Arts Context* (Rehnke 1987), chapters focus on issues related to assessment, market forces, mission reviews, planning processes, and procedures for accreditation and certification. As the editor notes, the book may be used in several different ways, but its main focus is on questions relating to the process of determining whether or not a specific career program should be added: How will the tenured liberal arts faculty react to the new program and new faculty? Does the program need to be accredited? What legal issues will be involved? How do we ensure that a high-quality program is developed that will meet the needs and standards of the profession?

The key distinction that must be made when reviewing the literature on ''innovations'' in higher education is that the implementation of an innovation and the initiation of an innovation are vastly different. As noted, the implementation of innovations usually is concerned with various instructional practices and how to get teachers to adopt new methods or technologies. The research accordingly focuses on the analysis of specific case studies to identify impediments to adoption. The initiation of innovation deals with the development of new products (from procedures to programs) and is largely an internal function, a process that ranges from the generation of an idea to its institutionalization. The process and procedures, the actors, the politics, and the dynamics are considerably different, depending on which of the two forms of innovation is being studied.

The key distinction that must be made when reviewing the literature on ''innovations'' in higher education is that the implementation of an innovation and the initiation of an innovation are vastly different.

Strategies for Innovation

While previous sections have concentrated on specific aspects of innovation in organizations, including colleges and universities, it should also be noted that mechanisms to implement change have been broadly investigated. These strategies are based upon the fact that knowledge of impediments or the understanding of a product's attributes is not enough. Coordinated planning procedures are required to negotiate the maze of complex organizations. A number of different classifications of "strategies for change" have been suggested. One classification scheme, for example, has three categories (Chin and Benne 1985, pp. 58–59). The first is a series of *empirical/ rational* approaches that involve convincing people by rational means, disseminating information derived from basic and applied research, and appealing to reason and logic. The second category, *normative/reeducative* strategies, involves attempts to affect values and habits of individuals and groups. Such approaches are directed toward altering existing organizational norms. The final category is *power/coercive* strategies. Such strategies attempt to bring about change through the use of economic, political, legal, and moral sanctions. Others follow a similar classification scheme involving three categories—*empirical rational, manipulative,* and *power*—in developing a typology of strategies for change in education (Zaltman et al. 1977, p. 81). The empirical rational approach proceeds by communicating the justification for change, the manipulative strategy attempts to rearrange features of the environment, and the power approach revolves around the threat or application of rewards and punishment.

More recently, a fivefold classification has been proposed that includes the various categories (rational, normative, and power) and adds another dimension related to the degree of outsider versus insider control over innovation (Hewton 1982). This classification includes the following strategies:

- *Participative problem solving* involves innovation controlled by local people, in which change is brought about in response to their needs, using local resources and self-help (control remains with insiders).
- *Open input* is a broad and flexible approach in which attempts are made to make full use of all ideas and resources from both inside and outside the local community

(control will vary according to which resources are used and for what purpose).

- *Power* concerns innovations that are clearly directed from above, using laws, formal procedures, a chain of command, and designated agents for technical assistance to bring about change (outsider control).
- *Diffusion* relates to innovations that are spread mainly through the media and through informal networks of opinion (messages fed into these networks are essentially those of outsiders).
- *Planned linkage* relies upon careful planning and the specification of clear goals and objectives related to a detailed analysis of the insiders' actual situation (considerable input from outsiders but attention is devoted to securing cooperation between insiders and outsiders) (p. 24).

While characteristics of the process, the people, and the product of an innovation are essentially descriptive in nature, strategies are the action plans that lead to adoption and eventually institutionalization. Such action planning is necessary in the management of change. But it should be noted that the strategies that have been outlined in these classifications do not describe mutually exclusive categories. Any major change that occurs in a complex organization like a college or university usually requires a combination of approaches.

Summary
The modern U.S. college or university is both a symbol of the past and a harbinger of the future—an organization that values its heritage and at the same time has a responsibility to be a catalyst for change. While innovation in higher education is requisite to its very existence, the nature of that innovation is therefore necessarily distinctive, and the movement is glacial: "Every advance in education is made over the dead bodies of 10,000 resisting professors" (Robert M. Hutchins, quoted in Jellema 1986, p. 9).

Higher education systems are not planned, staffed, financed, built, or programmed (except for a few experimental efforts) to do more than continue the traditional approach. Even when individual philosophers, behavior theorists, architects, economists, developmental psychologists, or engineers have

*managed to influence this system, their efforts have not sig-
nificantly affected the overall inertia in higher education institutions* (Evans 1982, p. 96).

It is evident that for our colleges and universities to progress,
as they have done for centuries, they must change. At the same
time, however, our institutions would be derelict in their obligation to society if they only mimicked the fads and fashions of
society. The success of this academic tightrope act depends
upon the ability of the institutions to filter meaningful innovation from whimsy. While the disciplines have proceeded
through gigantic leaps and dramatic shifts, the institutions have
proceeded incrementally. Recently, however, the need to generate innovative curricula has been linked to the fact that "the
acceleration of change in society is placing an even greater pre-
mium on new methods of knowledge transfer" (Lynton 1983,
p. 53). The acceleration of societal change may force colleges
and universities to consider alternative mechanisms to the incremental methods of yesterday. In a knowledge-intensive society, institutions of higher education cannot rely on detachment,
autonomy, and isolation to filter change. The link needs to be
more direct and more responsive:

*We must, in a conscious way, develop a much more sym-
biotic interaction with the world around us. This will require
a two-way flow of communications with a wide variety of
constituencies, leading to a sharing of responsibility for decisions in many areas [that] to date we have solely considered
our own domain. Obvious examples are program planning,
curriculum development, and even the time, mode, and location of our offerings* (Lynton 1983, p. 53).

Perhaps one of the most important observations that can be
made regarding the literature on innovation in higher education
is that it has not been directly applied to the development of
new academic programs. For example, while the critical distinction between initiation of innovation and implementation of
innovation is applicable to teaching and technological innovations, it has limited application to the development of new
academic programs. Specifically, the implementation of innovation, or the actual use of the innovation by members of the
organization, is meaningless when it comes to new academic
programs. A more useful distinction would be innovation initia-

tion, innovation impression, and innovation institutionalization. In this scheme, initiation involves the process of generating ideas and development at the level of the operating unit—a professor or group of professors. The process must eventually leave a "visible effect on the surface"; hence, innovation impression is the internal administrative process and external confirmation process required to get the program approved. Finally, institutionalization of innovation is that part of the process in which the college or university community accepts the program as a legitimate and viable entity.

In sum:

1. We need to develop a better understanding of the fact that innovation will be a function of organizational structure (e.g., size or complexity), organizational culture (i.e., general attitudes and norms toward change), the characteristics of change agents and targets, and the object of innovation. In short, we need to accept the idea that successful innovation of new academic programs is a messy business, filled with fits and starts, near misses, hurt feelings, resentment, and failures. Accept it. It is the very nature of change itself.

2. Higher education has been largely a closed and stable system. Consequently, such notions as "outside threats" and "vested interests" are particularly strong deterrents to innovation. Colleges and universities must continue a recent trend in looking outward. Such mechanisms as advisory boards, faculty consulting, service and joint programs, and interinstitutional cooperation need to be encouraged and rewarded. All such efforts, both large and small, tend to create an environment in which the development of new academic programs is a necessary element for the long-term vitality of the institution.

3. Equalization of power and the lack of institutional norms are functions of the decentralized structure in colleges and universities. Individual units, especially when resources are limited, will resist any innovation that remotely threatens the status quo. Decentralization results in a diffused set of norms with limited influence. Limited coercion can be used in such a decentralized structure to eliminate such decisiveness. But while "loners" can create and innovate in relatively peaceful isolation, they can become frustrated by the eventual politicking. Innovators

of academic programs must be encouraged but at the same time sheltered.

4. As higher education goes through cycles of fiscal constraint and relative wealth, it must be consistent in its belief and support for innovation. A college or university operates in a people-intensive environment with three-fourths of its budget tied up in salaries and fringe benefits. It simply does not have the fiscal flexibility of a manufacturing firm. A tendency might evolve therefore to resort to knee-jerk reactions to such pressure by deferring maintenance and declaring hiring freezes. "Retrenchment" is seen as a phase where the entire institution takes one giant step backward. Yet such across-the-board measures actively discourage the development of new academic programs, the very mechanism that can help resolve the down cycle.

5. The distinction between "initiation," "impression," and "institutionalization" is critical to the development of new academic programs in higher education. The processes and procedures that relate to effective initiation are quite different from those that relate to administrative program approval and acceptance on campus. Initiation of innovation, for example, flourishes in a complex, informal, decentralized environment—in a discipline-structured environment. Innovation impression does not. Effective program approval processes require simplicity, formalization, and centralization.

6. To facilitate initiation of innovation, colleges and universities need to concentrate on horizontal "integrating mechanisms." Such mechanisms are the people-means to stimulating initiation of innovation. Interdisciplinary teams, task forces, and team teaching are some of the means for combining ideas from unconnected sources. Such forums help to break down the isolation, fragmentation, and narrow bias that often characterize individual operating units. Any approach that can be used to generate cross-disciplinary communication and experimentation needs to be explored and encouraged.

7. To facilitate innovation impression, colleges and universities need to concentrate on vertical "structural links." The emphasis needs to shift from the understructure (the operating units) and the middlestructure (the administration) to the superstructure (the links between the two).

Regardless of where the idea for a new program is initiated, it cannot succeed without having negotiated the distance *between* the structures in an academic system. It must evolve from an idea to a well-defined description that can be evaluated on the basis of specific criteria.

8. To facilitate institutionalization of innovation, a new academic program must again concentrate on horizontal "integrating mechanisms." Once it has evolved from an idea to a formalized program that has been scrutinized by both internal and external members of the institution and its governing board, the program faces the problem of becoming accepted. It must compete for funding and students, and it must produce results that meet its goal statements. It needs to gain acceptance as a legitimate enterprise in an organizational structure that thrives on special interests and "turfmanship."

It is evident that these observations signal a need for an entirely different approach to innovation in higher education. We need an approach that steps beyond the individual department, an approach that is actively orchestrated across disciplines and functions at all levels of the institution. It is an approach that calls for various types of horizontal and vertical information flow. It requires leadership, risk taking, the cultivation of a change-accepting environment, and solid planning.

Definitions and Delineations

The terminology used to describe various aspects of academic programming can be more than a little confusing. Perhaps the broadest terms, and at the same time the most specific terms, that have been generally employed have been "curriculum planning" and "curriculum development." On the one hand, some references to the curriculum are concerned with curriculum planning that provides a framework and a philosophy for the organization of courses. Such recent documents as *A Nation at Risk, To Reclaim a Legacy, Involvement in Learning*, and *Integrity in the Undergraduate Curriculum* have debated the future structure of the undergraduate curriculum. On the other hand, when professors and administrators use terminology about curriculum development, they are often referring to the addition, deletion, and alteration of specific coursework within an academic unit.

"Program evaluation" is also used extensively in higher education. In the most general sense, evaluation is "a study that is designed and conducted to assist some audience to judge and improve the worth of some educational object" (Stufflebeam and Webster 1980, p. 6). A slightly more specific definition has been offered as well: "The term evaluation implies value judgments about the strengths and weaknesses of academic programs and, in addition, provides descriptive information about them" (M. Clark 1983, p. 27). It is possible to differentiate among four types of evaluation according to their aims:

1. Planning, or development, evaluation *is undertaken to determine needs or deficiencies and to devise objectives or goals to meet these needs.*
2. Input evaluation *aids in making decisions about how to use resources to attain program goals.*
3. Process evaluation *provides continuing or periodic feedback so that those responsible for program planning and operation can review and possibly alter earlier decisions.*
4. Output evaluation *assesses the attainment, at the end of a project or at appropriate stages within it, of those goals [that] are self-contained and of those [that] are preliminary to entering another stage* (Dressel 1976, pp. 15–16).

Most definitions and uses of "program evaluation" or "program assessment," therefore, refer to the application of various procedures to judge the quality of ongoing academic programs.

Knowing which new programs to introduce and when to introduce them greatly depends upon the strength and weaknesses of the current program portfolio.

Perhaps the most confusing term is "program review." In some people's minds, program review and program evaluation are synonymous. But while program evaluation is generally defined in broader terms, program review can take on several different scopes. One author recently described program review as "also known as 'program evaluation'—a rational and routine process for examining and strengthening ongoing programs" (Simpson 1985, p. 40). Such a definition obviously does not see program review as encompassing the development of new programs or the discontinuance of present programs. Others, in contrast, note that program review has been used variously to refer to decisions regarding the approval of programs or the continuation or even the demise of existing programs (Arns and Poland 1980, p. 268).

For the purpose of this section, "program review" will be used in a narrow context (ongoing programs), while "program evaluation" will be used in a broader context:

The process of specifying, defining, collecting, analyzing, and interpreting information about designated aspects of a given program, and using that information to arrive at value judgments among decision alternatives regarding the installation, continuation, modification, or termination of a program (Craven 1980, p. 434).

Several aspects of this definition are important. First, it includes references to the same subject matter that were used in the earlier definitions, that is, making judgments about programs based upon information. Second, it sees judgments as "decision alternatives," not just descriptive data. And finally, it sees academic programs in a temporal perspective; they come and go. Within this general definition of program evaluation, then, it is also able to refer to three separate stages: the development of new programs (installation), program review (continuation, modification), and program discontinuance (termination). The actual lines between these stages are blurred, and there is thus no clear delineation as to when or where each begins and the other ends. Specifically, the development of a new academic program requires not only the procedures necessary to get the program offered but may also require additional evaluation after its introduction to get it accredited. A program review, in addition, may or may not include mechanisms to begin the process of discontinuing a program that does not merit continued support. For the purposes of this report, however, it is especially important to differentiate these stages to see how the processes and procedures of "evaluation" relate to each other.

Which brings us to the title of this section. Academic program planning, as used in this report, is virtually synonymous with Craven's definition of program evaluation. The key elements of academic program planning are the following:

- It is a process and involves an ongoing series of actions.
- It is data based and requires both experiential and future-oriented information.
- It is related to the instructional program component—graduate, undergraduate, degree, and nondegree.
- It is a mechanism that requires choices and setting priorities.

This broad view of academic program planning, from program development to discontinuance, is important because it is the context within which program innovation occurs. Knowing which new programs to introduce and when to introduce them greatly depends upon the strength and weaknesses of the current program portfolio.

The Planning Environment
As we have previously seen, institutions of higher education have substantial mechanisms that enable them to change, to reflect societal shifts. But today's environment requires all organizations, colleges and universities included, to be more flexible and responsive than in the past.

Growth, constancy, and decline
One aspect of organizational flexibility that has received recent attention in the literature is the management of organizations of constant or decreasing size. Most organizational theory and research have been based on the assumption of growth—that more revenues, more assets are necessarily good (Whetten 1980). But the formulas, structures, and policies that are used for planning in times of growth are often ill suited as mechanisms for managing constancy or decline; in response, a substantial literature has emerged in business, public affairs, and hospital administration (Cameron, Kim, and Whetten 1987). The basic bias in all of these organizations comes from the

concentration on the business firm where the motivation is always for increasing sales, increasing production, and increasing profits. The resulting implicit assumption is that most organizations are either expanding or are interested in expanding.

Beginning with Cyert (1978), some attention has also been paid to the issue in higher education. The driving force behind this sudden interest is manifold. One factor is the downturn in the demographic cycle of high school seniors, another is the increasing costs of higher education (especially private institutions), and another is decreasing federal support for student aid. At present, most colleges and universities would be pleased if they could be assured of an institution of constant size through the end of this century.

Since 1870 enrollments in higher education have grown at a compound annual rate of 5 percent, ahead of the total population growth of 1.6 percent. Resources used by institutions of higher education have increased from what we estimate was 0.1 percent of the GNP in 1870 to 2.1 percent presently (not including construction). During the next 20 years, enrollments may fall even as the total population continues to rise; real resources available to and used by colleges and universities also may decline, even if and as the total GNP keeps increasing. This dramatic new situation has given rise to a great sense of uncertainty within higher education, to many fears and to some hopes (Carnegie Council 1980, p. 1).

The vision of constancy or decline is important to higher education because colleges and universities are especially vulnerable to shrinking resources. Their vulnerability lies in their lack of mechanisms for managing such a downturn. While faculty unions and accreditation groups that function as external advocates for ever-increasing resources can be obstructions to managed decline, the main hindrance is structure. Higher education's decentralized structure operates effectively in a growth environment because limited central action is required. Without a strong hierarchical structure, however, periods of constancy or decline are problematic. Tough choices need to be made and implemented: "Postsecondary institutions remain ponderous creatures with decentralized decision making, high fixed costs, and few successful attempts at program restructure or curtailment" (Gillis 1982, p. 33). Perhaps the most stark description of the negative impact that loosely coupled systems have on responsiveness is the following one:

> *Decision making becomes an escalating series of major compromises that frequently prevent any final decision. Within the institution, faculty members tend to view major problems from individual viewpoints and normally attempt to assure a decision that will minimize interruption of their activities. Furthermore, the internal decision-making structure is designed to approve rather than disapprove courses, programs, institutions, centers, and other encumbrances that add to educational as well as administrative costs. Faculty members sit on overseer committees and frequently waive, rather than enforce, rules designed to reduce costs. Thus, the governance structure of universities thwarts tough-minded decisions, encourages expansion, and hinders an overall perspective* (Tucker and Mautz 1980, p. 40).

And while the problem of constraints on resources may be only temporary (for the next eight to ten years perhaps), the nature of colleges and universities is anything but temporary. Tucker and Mautz's remarks are of the 1980s, but they reach the same conclusion that another author reached almost 60 years ago: "The besetting sin of our institutions is their insatiable impulse to expand materially" (Holt 1930, p. 503).

The rigidity and inaction that have been described can often lead to a series of vicious circles in a contracting organization. One study of 334 institutions of higher education concluded that when decline is present, the organization is characterized by more leaders made scapegoats, low morale, fragmented pluralism, resistance to change, and curtailment of innovation (Cameron, Kim, and Whetten 1987). Long-term planning is often abandoned in favor of ad hoc decision making. As the institution retracts within itself, protecting individual territories, it becomes less aware of environmental threats and opportunities. Subunits become interested only in survival and preserving the status quo—going unnoticed and, one hopes, untouched as well. The ability to develop new initiatives, so critical in an environment of changing knowledge, is greatly impaired. Gaining flexibility through internal reallocation is nearly impossible as the individual units "hunker down." And as the institution becomes increasingly parochial and lethargic, it can lose its distinctiveness and its appeal. The result is a continued downturn, a vicious circle.

But to maintain quality and improve itself, a contracting organization must find a new mix of services (Cyert 1978). The process of identifying internal strengths and weaknesses and external threats and opportunities becomes the vehicle for managing the transition from growth to constancy or decline. It is a transition that requires innovation, not stagnation, in academic planning.

Methods and means

Within higher education, planning has always been a primary function of institutional administrators. Such planning has been undertaken at three different levels. The first level concerns budgeting and scheduling and is requisite to the operation of any organization. A second level focuses on short-range planning and entails such areas of concern as recruiting students, decisions about the physical plant, and program (curricular) modifications. Long-range planning represents the final level. This type of planning involves five- and ten-year blueprints based largely upon quantitative models (Kotler and Murphy 1981, p. 471).

"Strategic planning" has a considerably different orientation and has been contrasted with long-range planning (Cope 1981). Strategic planning can be described as an open system, using external (qualitative) information to develop an understanding of a dynamic process. Long-range planning is, instead, a closed system, using internal (quantitative) information to develop a static blueprint. Perhaps the most parsimonious definition is strategic planning as "the process of developing and maintaining a strategic fit between the organization and its changing marketing opportunities" (Kotler and Murphy 1981, p. 481).

According to one recent survey (Clugston 1986), the literature on strategic planning in higher education has grown exponentially. While fewer than six articles appeared in the literature before 1978, since then 168 have dealt with strategic planning, management, and higher education (see, for example, Balderston 1981, Peterson 1980, and Uhl 1983). This sudden interest in strategic planning can be traced to a number of environmental factors. First and most important is lack of growth. As previously noted, during periods of growth most priorities are met through additional available resources. Whatever cuts are made are not politically sensitive or vulnerable to second-guessing. The assumption of a dynamic environment and the decision-making orientation of strategic planning make it especially topical in periods of instability (Salloway and Tack 1978, p. 2). In addition to demographic and economic factors that affect patterns of growth, a strong political reason also exists for adopting strategic planning procedures. Failure to develop proactive institutional planning procedures invites the imposition of state- or board-generated plans and procedures. By implementing their own plans, colleges and universities can maintain control over their destinies and, more immediately, the daily choices that must be made among different alternatives. And finally, one cannot discount the need to compete: One has only to note that proprietary schools and corporate education programs are diverting more students from traditional four-year programs and that community colleges and public institutions are drawing students seeking lower-priced alternatives to private colleges.

To draw the topics of academic program planning and strategic planning closer together, it is useful to enumerate the basic characteristics of strategic planning as they relate to general notions regarding academic programming (see table 1). The application of strategic planning can only aid in the process of installing, continuing, modifying, or terminating academic programs (Tack, Rentz, and Russell 1984).

Strategic planning is very much a framework for action. Its intellectual roots are found in policy research, marketing, and effectiveness research (Cope 1981, p. 2). As such, it is concerned with matching organizational characteristics and output with clients or customers. This process of seeking a distinct "match" results in a college or university's actively positioning itself within the pattern of all higher education institutions. The action framework involves several guiding principles. The first is the notion of comparative advantage. Looking inward, the organization needs to identify, nurture, and exploit its special capabilities. For a college or university, this comparative advantage may come from its location, the physical beauty of its campus, or specific programs and professors. The second principle is the concept of "niche." By matching internal "comparative advantages" with one or more segments of the market, a position of strength is established. "Niches" could include older, returning students, corporate executives, and so on (Cyert 1981, p. 35). A whole range of tactics, models, and tools can be used to operationalize strategic planning. Two of

TABLE 1

CHARACTERISTICS OF STRATEGIC PLANNING RELATED TO PROGRAM PLANNING

Strategic Planning	Program Planning
1. Its perspective is of the organization or subunit as a whole, involving decisions cutting across departments and functions.	*Program planning must by definition entail comparisons of programs across various disciplines.*
2. It places great emphasis on the conditions of the environment, seeking to match institutional capabilities with environmental conditions to achieve goals.	*Program planning decisions should be based upon the external impact of the choices as well as cross-discipline comparisons.*
3. It is an iterative, continuing learning process.	*All programs that a higher education institution offers, or will be offering, must be subject to continual adaptation—including possible termination.*
4. It is more concerned with doing the right thing than with doing things right. It is more concerned with effectiveness than efficiency.	*The specific rules and regulations of program planning are secondary to a more important factor—the quality of the value judgments made among decision alternatives.*

Source: Adapted from Cope 1981, p. 6.

these applications are useful to the organization of the remainder of this section—product life cycle and the product portfolio matrix.

The standard product life cycle is an S-shaped curve that is divided into four segments—introduction, growth, maturation, and decline. Most of the research on product life cycles has been performed by marketers who have developed a set of strategies that coincide with the different stages. All products and product classes go through a life cycle. Fads last a few months, while traditional items may last hundreds of years without substantial change. The metaphor of life cycle has also been used to describe organizational changes (Cameron, Kim, and Whetten 1987) and seen some limited application in higher

TABLE 1 (*continued*)

**CHARACTERISTICS OF STRATEGIC PLANNING
RELATED TO PROGRAM PLANNING**

Strategic Planning	Program Planning
5. It seeks to maximize synergistic effects, i.e., making two plus two equal five.	*The process of interpreting information generated by broad-based review committees and external consultants brings multiple energies to program planning.*
6. It seeks to answer the question, What is our mission, role, and scope, and what should be our mission, role, and scope? That is, what business are we in and what business should we be in?	*A key criterion in measuring the viability of a new program venture has to be "centrality to mission."*
7. It is concerned with the basic character of the organization, the core of special competence.	*Program prestige and long-run viability are based upon its ability to carry out the institutional mission in a distinctly professional fashion.*
8. Its emphasis is on change, review, reexamination. It is not static.	*Innovation is essential to the health of academic programming.*

Source: Adapted from Cope 1981, p. 6.

education (e.g., Baldridge 1980). The obvious use of the concept of product life cycle in higher education is contained in the correspondence between the life cycle stages and Craven's decision alternatives enumerated in his definition of program evaluation—installation (introduction), continuation (growth), modification (maturation), and termination (decline). The literature in higher education has developed around the three sets of policies and procedures relative to program approval, program review, and program discontinuance. *Perhaps the most important principles involved in the metaphor of life cycle as they relate to higher education are that products (programs) will necessarily decline so that introducing new products (programs) is critical to long-run survival, that products (programs) must be managed through their entire cycle, and that it is important to recognize where in the life cycle each product (program) is and to consider the related strategies.*

The product portfolio matrix and portfolio analysis are ways to combine product management and resource allocation. Viewing an organization as a multiproduct, multimarket conglomeration results in a matrix or grid that can be useful in making strategic choices. Each product, or business, within the organization is assigned to one of four matrix cells based upon its characteristics of market growth and market share: "stars," those with good growth potential and market share; "cash cows," those with weak growth potential but good market share; "question marks," those with high growth potential but poor market share; and "dogs," those with poor prospects and poor market share. Very briefly, dogs should be phased out and the residual capital steered to the stars for nourishment (Abell and Hammond 1979). A number of authors have applied portfolio analysis to academic programs as just described (e.g., Foster 1983), others have altered the axes to reflect student demand and program quality (Keller 1983), and still others have expanded the grid to include additional categories (Gillis 1982). *The most important principles of portfolio analysis as applied to higher education are that products (programs) are scrutinized for their current performance and potential, that the analysis is comparative, requiring judgments about a product (program) compared to its competition, and that constancy in resources is assumed, thereby forcing the organization to fuel innovation through the reallocation of resources.*

Program Review

While it would be reasonable to begin the next three sections with "development of new programs," the logical order has been altered for several reasons. First, just as with maturity in the product life cycle, most program evaluation is done in the form of program review, that is, the evaluation of existing programs for the purpose of improvement (modification and continuation). The obvious explanation for it is that comparatively few new programs (or products) are added or deleted each year as a percentage of all the programs (or products) offered. The second reason for examining program review first is that the bulk of the literature on program evaluation deals with considerations about program review. Our interest in program review, and program discontinuance as well, is only from the perspective of their being forms of evaluation—as is the development of new programs. While a full review of these topic areas is far beyond the scope of this report, our interest in them is focused on the manner in which each relates to the others as part of strategic planning and program planning. Consequently, this review is limited to an analysis of the extent to which issues on table 1 are examined and discussed in the literature. Further, it is important to highlight any references in these three areas that see program planning in ongoing (product life cycle) terms and in terms of setting priorities (portfolio analysis).

A number of recent books on program review are excellent. One is a descriptive study of program review practice, both within a college or university and at the system or state level (Barak 1982). Another, prescriptive in nature, emphasizes procedures for designing program reviews (Wilson 1982). And still another describes the approaches to program review and the major issues involved (Conrad and Wilson 1985). Case studies of procedures for program review at specific institutions are also abundant (see, e.g., M. Clark 1983 for reports on eight case studies). The vastly increased attention given in recent years to program review as a component of program planning efforts has been discussed in the literature as well. There is little doubt that the heightened level of attention given to program review has been greatly influenced by state governments and by governing and coordinating boards. Concerns about quality, effectiveness and efficiency, and accountability have been the slogans used to promote *external* program review. The driving force behind such activities is the perceived need for more accountability using quantitative measures and outside consultants (Folger 1977). While numbers of articles have described the processes and procedures involved in state-level program review (see, e.g., Miller and Barak 1986), minimal attention appears to have been given to strategic planning or more comprehensive issues of program planning. Concerns about duplicating programs and a tie-in with master planning are mentioned in a strategic sense, but usually the process is mechanistic and bureaucratic in nature—which is not to say that such procedures are a waste of time, for they do serve a very important function of "accountability."

Some of the interest in and pressure for program review have come from the campus community because of concerns about program quality and the need to reallocate funds under conditions of fiscal pressure (Groves 1979, p. 1). While the administration is in the best position to make strategic use of program

Without the fiscal pressure, department-based program reviews have been internal mechanisms to make incremental improvements in quality.

review, historically it has not been the case. Without the fiscal pressure, department-based program reviews have been internal mechanisms to make incremental improvements in quality. The current interest in program review, however, is strongly dictated by fiscal considerations: "If resources were not constrained, there would be insufficient motivation to endure the anxieties of unsparing self-assessment and the conflicts arising from the decision to replace old programs with new ventures" (Simpson 1985, p. 40). Such an observation, that program review be linked to the reallocation of funds to initiate new or to expand high-demand programs, is a strong endorsement of a portfolio approach to academic program planning. This shift from seeing internal program review as being synonymous with just "program improvement" toward an orientation that includes strategic choices can be seen in several case examples:

- The chancellor of the University of Indiana noted that a comprehensive programmatic review and planning process enables the institution to establish priorities. In fact, he noted that after the review process has been completed, each unit should consider (1) what existing support services or academic programs should be left unchanged, (2) what existing support services or academic programs should be modified, (3) what existing support services or academic programs should be phased out, and (4) what new support services or academic programs should be offered (Thompson 1986, p. 5).
- An expanded program review process at the University of Kansas served an important function through the "development of an understanding of where programs and departments might have flexibility or where programmatic flexibility might exist" (Breier 1986, p. 17).
- At the University of Illinois, the rationale for linking academic plans with program reviews was to "bring both activities under a single campus decision-making structure (the academic planning committee), thereby ensuring that the status of existing programs would be considered in the planning of new programs" (Groves 1979, p. 6).

These examples make it apparent that some institutions have begun to think of program review as an ongoing, data-based system to enable them to make choices regarding academic programs. Contributions of program review to strategic planning in colleges and universities are enumerated in table 2.

Two concerns need to be discussed based upon the literature of program review. While recent research, writings, and case examples do indicate a more strategic orientation, it does not appear that mere data are sufficient to generate actions by themselves. A recent survey of states' reviews of undergraduate academic programs found that demand, quality, program duplication, need, mission compatibility, and costs (in that order) were the crucial criteria, with similar criteria being used internally by the institutions (Miller and Barak 1986). Many of the strategic choices that are implied in such notions as reallocation, setting priorities, competitive advantage, and the determination of institutional strengths and weaknesses require a synthesis of data. Isolated criteria applied to singular program reviews do not provide the coordinated, institutionwide perspective that is necessary to generate change. And without such comprehensive decision making, the result can be the institutional equivalent of a rocking chair—much activity but no movement.

Perhaps part of this skepticism is based upon the second concern. While many well-intentioned administrators may have responded to fiscal exigencies and external pressure by designing broad-based program reviews, the culture of colleges and universities has not quite caught up. As program review has come

TABLE 2
CONTRIBUTIONS OF PROGRAM REVIEW TO STRATEGIC PLANNING

1. Helps to contribute to overall institutional effectiveness.
2. Helps to identify institutional priorities.
3. Helps in budgeting and reallocation.
4. Helps to give faculty, administration, and board of trustees a sense of good stewardship.
5. Helps define institutional mission.
6. Helps assess an institution's competitive advantage.
7. Helps provide guidance for program improvement.
8. Helps to determine institutional strengths and weaknesses.
9. Helps provide for institutional accountability (i.e., improved external relations).
10. Helps contribute to overall institutional quality.

Source: Barak 1986, p. 17.

to mean something more than a passive, internal exercise, it has also generated some bad press among departments. "In the modern context . . . if the words 'program review' are mentioned by a college president, the response is similar to that within the Lord Executioner's court: Departments duck and hope the ax will fall elsewhere" (Simpson 1985, p. 40). Given this context, the issues discussed earlier regarding culture, structure, and organizational decision making are of great concern in translating criteria and data into strategic choices. These two bodies of literature, organizational culture and strategic planning, have not been adequately integrated in higher education.

Program Discontinuance
While program discontinuance is a stage of the academic planning process and a natural extension of program review, it has nonetheless generated its own body of literature. While most people think of program discontinuance as the outright elimination of a program, it can also include the merger of related programs, the elimination of certain degrees or programs within departments, and the closing of entire departments (Melchiori 1982). Discontinuance is, in fact, a series of steps that extends a program review to include initiating program discontinuance, the review process itself, including the selection of models and evaluation criteria, making decisions, implementing the decision, and assessing impacts on students, faculty, academic programs, institutional budgets, and organizational behavior.

Much of the research and writings in this area have focused on the specific criteria to be used. Heightened attention is given to this topic because the consequences of standard program reviews do not necessarily result in the elimination of the program. Given the highly political aspects of program discontinuance, it is therefore reasonable that some authors have scrutinized the criteria (see, e.g., Brown 1970 and Mayhew 1979). The guidelines generally include such items as demand, costs, placement record of graduates, external funding, critical mass, competition, quality, and, perhaps most important, the centrality of the program to the institution's core mission (Lincoln and Tuttle 1983). Again, some case examples view program discontinuance in terms of strategic choices:

- At California State University–Dominguez Hills, programs' viability was discussed in terms of the problem of "how to continue program development on a campus not yet fully developed—add new programs, renew or maintain others, allow others to grow, even phase out some—while sustaining a net loss of some 22 faculty positions and related resources" (Karber and MacPhee 1980, p. 28).

- The planning process, objectives, and procedures used by Duke University's chancellor emphasized enhancing the university's strengths while reducing costs in ways that included phasing out programs (Franklin 1982).
- A planning approach implemented at the University of Minnesota emphasized the successful reduction of programs to achieve positive goals. The key elements in this process were the use of definitive criteria for making decisions to justify priorities that were important to strategic planning (Mason 1984).
- Planning by the University of Wisconsin system included the notion that the elimination or consolidation of marginal programs was one of an array of choices. Further, a change in a college or university's mission may be an instrument for enabling a particular institution to evolve (Smith 1980).

A number of concerns in the literature on program discontinuance are related to the general topic of academic program planning. One such concern is the very real problem that, for many in higher education, program discontinuance is the same as retrenchment. Most administrators and faculty members approach program reduction as a budget issue; that is, without fiscal exigency, program discontinuance is not a necessary action. While eliminating a program is one strategy that is often considered during times of budget constraints, it is only one of many possible strategies—for example, across-the-board cuts, deferral of maintenance, hiring freezes, generating revenue (Mingle 1982). And while program discontinuance may be caused by budgetary problems, the product life cycle model and portfolio approaches to strategic planning do not assume fiscal exigency. By equating retrenchment and program discontinuance, the ongoing critical judgment of programs becomes something less than a strategic planning process. This reactive, defensive approach to program review is obvious in the words of advice offered by one author: "Extreme care should be taken to avoid adding programs or significant expense while the process of elimination is in process" (Mayhew 1979, p. 273).

It should also be mentioned that the analogy of the rocking chair may be even more applicable when it comes to program discontinuance. At West Virginia University, for example, a $400,000, two-year study project provided the basis for numerous strategic planning decisions. Internally, program reviews—with broad participation by faculty—produced hundreds of recommendations for improving the university's 16 schools and colleges (Academy 1984). Actual cutbacks, however, including suspension or reduction of about a third of the university's 48 doctoral programs, generated "incredible resistance." Program review and program discontinuance cannot have any strategic value without incorporating a detailed understanding of the culture, structure, and decision-making context of the organization when changes are required.

The Development of New Academic Programs

Of the three areas of program planning, the development of new academic programs has seen the least attention, but perhaps the most instructive work is offered in Barak 1982. That comprehensive study of program review devotes two chapters to program approval—one to internal mechanisms and the other to approving programs at the system and state levels. Barak uses survey data to describe criteria, participants, and procedures in the program approval process. A much more prescriptive study details an eight-stage procedure for developing new programs in institutions of higher education (Lee and Gilmour 1977). The stages, which range from "definition of institutional mission and service area" to "program evaluation," are an adaptation and extension of the six stages of new product development described in the business literature.

It would appear that the lack of attention to this aspect of academic program planning is directly related to the growth orientation of colleges and universities. The structure and culture of institutions of higher education are slanted toward adding, not subtracting. Involved discussions of program priorities or mechanisms that enable decision makers to choose between alternatives are not particularly relevant when the environment will support nondecisions. "The climate is 'live and let live.' A decision that dismisses a faculty member, closes a program, or diverts students is an attack upon us all, collectively and individually. Hari-kari is not part of our culture; deferred maintenance is" (Tucker and Mautz 1980, p. 41). Consequently, decisions about new programs have not been subjected to critical review because they have been largely a function of increased budgets (Gaff 1980). As long as the numbers (students, tuition, state funding, endowments, federal and foundation research grants) were on the rise, new programs would necessarily follow. But the environment has changed. A "niggardly environment" (Benveniste 1985) means that higher education faces strong competition for local funds, an economic malaise, and rising costs associated with a labor-intensive enterprise. But continuing with business as usual in such an environment can have a detrimental effect on institutional operations. For example, a recent master plan assessment by the Missouri State Coordinating Board (1983) revealed that over the 10 years from 1972 to 1982, the net number of new programs increased by 31.8 percent—while the total degrees awarded during the same period remained almost unchanged. "While this phenomenon greatly increased geographic access, consequences of this activity have also included highly segmented curricula, narrowly focused professional programs at the baccalaureate level, and a multiplicity of low productivity programs" (p. 37).

Given this state of affairs, the importance of a more strategic approach to adding new programs is obvious. Under conditions of constancy or decline, any new initiatives must be a function of internal shifts and reordered priorities. Specific analyses of the strengths and weaknesses of ongoing programs must be balanced against new opportunities in a dynamic environment. The reallocation of resources must be part of an integrative framework that actively seeks to make continual adjustments to maintain quality while fueling innovation. Several case examples emphasize this theme:

- In a study of five colleges and universities, ratios of undergraduates per program, faculty members per program, and budget per program were calculated for 1975 and 1985. While the number of new programs increased significantly, the other ratios decreased over the 10-year period. The conclusion: Popular or relevant programs are developed—some of which are probably appropriate to the mission of the institution, others of which are not. Few, if any, programs are dropped. Resources, budgetary and personnel, are stretched to meet new needs while causing many existing programs to survive on a subsistence level.

This forced-resource diet jeopardizes both the quality of the stronger programs and the future needs of the newly added programs.*

- A case study of Grambling State University (Lundy 1985) involved the use of planning tools to evaluate the economic consequences of implementing new programs. Cost-volume-revenue analysis, cost behavior analysis and least squares, and differential analysis were deemed useful to a "careful integration of academic, fiscal, and facilities planning before new programs are implemented" (p. 32).

Given the cost of this incremental investment in new programs, it is also obvious that great care must be taken in choosing which opportunities to explore. New is not necessarily better. And the practice of committing additional resources to unproven programs only feeds the paranoia of faculty members and departments who fear the budgetary axe. The ensuing arguments are much akin to those witnessed on a national level when funds are poured into foreign aid while, at the same time, we face a myriad of economic problems at home. New programs must be supremely defendable under such conditions (Benveniste 1985, p. 182).

Summary
Strategic planning is a way of thinking—a way of going about daily tasks that encourages options, a competitive outlook, futurism, and, above all else, decision making. As for innovation, a strategic orientation fosters an entrepreneurial spirit that encourages a certain amount of daring—an aggressive pursuit of new opportunities. A clear and focused strategy enables a college or university to take more calculated, necessary risks to enhance the long-term viability and quality of the institution and its programs (Keller 1983, p. 142).

Authors agree generally that institutions of higher education need to plan well. Care must be taken to examine the external environment, and greater attention is being focused on the assessment of the strengths and weaknesses of existing programs. Above all, colleges and universities must keep a keen vigilance for opportunities to provide additional service to society (Hollowood 1981, p. 8). An important observation to make, however,

---

*Information from author's unpublished study, 1988.

is that the development of opportunities in the form of new programs cannot continue as a random function of a growth environment. A more comprehensive, data-based approach is required to make tough choices between alternatives. The fact remains that virtually every program currently existing or about to be proposed in colleges and universities can make a strong case for funding. Treated in isolation, each can justify its own existence.

The three-stage life cycle of new program development, program review, and program discontinuance has been a useful way of organizing the literature about academic program planning. One way to look at these relationships is developed in table 3. As one proceeds through the five basic steps of stra-

TABLE 3
A DYNAMIC MODEL OF ACADEMIC/STRATEGIC PLANNING

Five-Step Strategic Planning Process	Review	Development and Discontinuance
1. Academic managers look at key trends in the environment and assess the threats and opportunities they pose.	-------->	
2. They assess their institution's strengths and weaknesses.	-------------->	
3. Based upon their institution's mission and the fit between their opportunities and strengths, they set a strategic direction.	---------------------->	
4. They set program priorities.	-------------------------------->	
5. They reallocate resources from low-priority to high-priority programs.	--------------------------------------->	

tegic "thinking," the steps evolve from strictly gathering data (step 1) to an orientation toward decisions (step 5). Much of academic program planning is concerned with evaluation in the form of program review, an information-intensive process. But while the review of existing programs usually results in only incremental adjustments, it is also the basis for more strategic decisions involving setting priorities, allocating resources, and eventually developing or discontinuing programs. As such, the importance of strategic thinking and the interrelationship of the three stages cannot be overemphasized.

A number of insights can be made from this review of the literature on academic programming and strategic planning as they pertain to the development of new academic programs:

1. As one academician has recently noted, program planning must transcend a preoccupation with the past and become an integral part of planning for the future (Benoist 1986, p. 22). We must also be willing to judge our efforts against several standards—not just internal comparisons of historical data. This narrow, parochial (and defensive) focus needs to broaden to include judgments about our programs based upon information regarding similar programs at other institutions and future trends within the discipline and the institutional environment.

2. The criticality of program review to the development of new programs has received minimal attention. Yet it has been noted that one of the positive contributions of program review is the increased consideration of alternative ways to develop and deliver programs (Barak 1986, p. 21). More specifically, "New program development and program improvement almost always grow out of evaluation processes" (Martens 1985, p. 8). Program review procedures provide the ongoing mechanisms to identify the strengths of the faculty and institutional programs. And as such, these procedures generate the essential information to guide the most decision-oriented phases of academic program planning (i.e., new program development and program discontinuance).

3. While it is important to nurture the link between program review and new program development, it should be recognized that such a link is complicated by a culture that in many cases has come to view program review as synonymous with program discontinuance. This attitude fos-

ters a defensiveness that necessarily constrains both faculty members and administrators in their honest efforts to audit the strengths and weaknesses of the current academic programming. Program review must therefore become an accepted part of campus culture.

4. One of the most vexing organizational paradoxes limiting the development of innovative new programs in higher education is that "during periods of abundance the resources to make major changes are present, but not the incentive, [and] during periods of scarcity the incentive is present, but not the resources" (Whetten 1984, p. 43). Many program discontinuances are "paper programs" resulting in no savings in resources and no additional flexibility. Other savings are of the nickel-and-dime variety—reducing travel funds or deferring maintenance. The development of new programs and the opportunity to leverage the strengths of the institution need to be seen as a function of institutional flexibility, not institutional growth.

5. Strong, centralized decision making is essential for program review and program discontinuance. Further, certain aspects of planned change in new program development, specifically the internal program approval process, also require simplicity, formalization, and centralization. But such aspects of program planning stand in stark contrast to both initiation of innovation and institutionalization of innovation in new program development, which thrive in an informal, decentralized environment. This "loose-tight" flexion is an important element in program development within the context of academic program planning.

Academic program planning can easily be viewed as a waste of time. Often it entails the generation of annual reports or program reviews that contain tables on student credit hours, course offerings, and headcounts. Faculty members' curricula vitae are pulled together, and the whole package is arranged so that it will stand upright on some administrator's shelf. One department may prepare an annual report, an accreditation report, and a program review (both institutional and system) all for the same time period. And the fact remains that nothing changes anyway. "Planning" in such an environment hardly approaches the definition of strategic planning offered earlier—"A process of developing and maintaining a strategic fit between the organization and its changing market opportunities.'' Yet planning, properly conducted, is the mechanism that enables an institution to make informed choices that allow excellence to triumph over mediocrity. When an incremental investment is made in an excellent program (new or ongoing), its reputation develops and spreads. It attracts more and better candidates from a wider radius, it has better success in hiring the best professors, and a pride in quality performance becomes the standard.

DECISIONS ABOUT THE DEVELOPMENT OF NEW ACADEMIC PROGRAMS

Major Considerations

The development of new academic programs can undoubtedly be considered in quite a number of different ways. From the initial inspiration—the idea—to final implementation often involves dozens of people over several years, and one can focus on the source of new ideas, evaluation methods, or the relationship of the people involved and the accompanying information network. Looking at new programs along a continuum from innovation to imitation is another approach. The development of new *products* has been researched from all these perspectives, but the development of new *programs* has not. One linear model has been particularly useful in the business literature; corporate designers, marketers, and comptrollers have come to view new product development as a decay curve from generation of an idea to commercialization. The standard eight-stage curve (Booz, Allen & Hamilton 1982) is a mechanism to enable the firm to go from a large number of ideas to the successful introduction of a new product by making a series of decisions (go, no go, get more information) over a period of time. The middle six stages include screening, concept development and testing, market strategy, business analysis, product development, and market testing.

It is readily apparent that the wholesale application of the new product development curve to academic programs is inappropriate.

It is readily apparent that the wholesale application of the new product development curve to academic programs is inappropriate. For one thing, industry experts estimate that only one successful product is developed out of every seven product ideas researched (Booz, Allen & Hamilton 1982). If academe's average were one out of seven, far fewer colleges and universities would be in operation today. As noted in the previous section, a variation of the new product development curve has been adapted to higher education. Lee and Gilmour's eight-stage procedure (1977) is designed "to provide institutional decision makers, planners, and faculty with a systematic approach for identifying ideas for new academic programs and for estimating the demand for these programs before they are implemented" (p. 305). Table 4 summarizes this procedure for academic program development. While all the stages have useful ideas, the procedure itself has not been used in higher education. Certainly one reason for this lack is that the development of new academic programs is too institution specific. It is not so much a sequential procedure in higher education as it is a series of looped iterations. Faculty members work with administrators to detail needs, staffing, and other concerns. Plans are changed, budgets are pared down, space requirements are altered, admission standards are revised. Program descriptors are pushed and pulled, and the process is repeated as administrators review their plans with state and system board members. It is a herky-jerky process and as such defies linear systematization.

An easy way to view the development of new academic programs, and thus review the literature, is by identifying the major inputs to decisions and the nature of the decisions themselves (Shirley and Volkwein 1978, p. 475). Internal considerations involve the assessment of strengths and capabilities; external needs and opportunities must be considered as well. Internally, the emphasis is on identifying the mechanisms to evaluate existing operations and resources. Externally, the emphasis shifts toward evaluation of the various constituencies. Decisions about campus programs and priorities are then made as a result of "matching" external needs, internal strengths, and institutional mission. Program approval at the state and system levels entails a final set of decisions about programs and priorities. These four sets of considerations in effect constitute the process of new program development.

Internal Strengths and Capabilities
Any successful organization is keenly aware of both its strengths and weaknesses. And while most of the organization's

TABLE 4
SUMMARY OF THE STAGES OF ACADEMIC PROGRAM PLANNING

1. *Definition:* What are the mission and service area?
2. *Idea generation:* Is the idea worth further development?
3. *Idea screening:* Is the idea compatible with institutional mission and resources?
4. *Concept development:* Can the idea be developed into an appealing program concept?
5. *Concept testing:* Is the program's concept sound and appealing? Will the program avoid duplication of others? Is outside funding available?
6. *Costing:* Will the program be too costly?
7. *Estimation of program demand:* Is there sufficient demand for the program?
8. *Program evaluation:* Should the program be implemented?

Source: Lee and Gilmour 1977, p. 307.

attention is necessarily devoted to the daily task of getting the product out the door, the underlying process that allows it to be competitive is the notion of maximizing strengths and minimizing weaknesses. The organization needs to understand the exact nature of its own capabilities or distinctive competencies to differentiate itself from other organizations and their products. In institutions of higher education, internal strengths and capabilities can range from a favorable student/faculty ratio to a beautiful campus. But the key assessment is the process of program evaluation that identifies what the college or university can do or, conversely, what it cannot do in quality fashion: "New program development and program improvement almost always grow out of evaluation processes" (Martens 1985, p. 15).

One way to think about this process is in terms of planning styles (Heydinger 1980a). These planning styles (developed from the literature on planning and from experience) are imprecise mechanisms and as such contrast to Lee and Gilmour's eight-stage interacting procedure. The styles are a taxonomy of overlapping approaches, and an institution relies on several such styles to develop new programs and plan ongoing programs. The first six styles focus on the constituency responsible for initiating or maintaining a program—that is, *who* is responsible for it. The second seven styles describe the planning process used—or *how* academic planning is done.

- *Knowledge development*: Curricula are developed as an unintentional by-product of research. For example, the discipline of computer science was added to the curriculum after the initial research on digital computing.
- *Entrepreneurial*: Faculty members come forward whenever they have an idea for altering or expanding academic programs in a laissez-faire, individual approach to program planning. No planning constraints, no timetables, and no formal requests for ideas are involved.
- *Administrative initiative*: Program planning ideas originate with academic administrators, who then may follow a variety of actions to have those plans implemented.
- *Curriculum committee*: Program development is either initiated or reviewed by a committee of faculty.
- *Governing/coordinating board*: The responsibility and initiative for planning and reviewing academic programs rests with the institution's governing board (trustees or regents, for example) or the state's coordinating board.

- *Formal democratic*: All units are requested to formulate their plans for program development in a cyclic planning process. Plans are reviewed simultaneously to arrive at an overall academic plan for the department, college, university, or system.

—ooo—

- *Problem focused*: Programs are planned "as needed"—whenever a problem arises or a distinct opportunity presents itself. Responsibility for initiating this process may rest with a number of constituencies, including some external to the institution.
- *Needs assessment*: Planning academic programs is guided by the needs of students, alumni, or employers. This information is collected through any number of social science research techniques.
- *Program data*: A comprehensive set of measures reflecting the current status and trends of academic programs is collected and collated. Such data are typically maintained by the office of institutional research and used by academic administrators to guide decisions about program planning.
- *Program review*: Strengths and weaknesses of existing academic programs are assessed in a retrospective process as a means for suggesting program development and improvement.
- *Program development fund*: Through a formal process of submitting proposals, ideas for program development are selected and awarded funds for implementation. This institutional process is analogous to applying for a grant from a private foundation.
- *Incremental budgeting*: Most decisions about academic program planning are made through this traditional budgeting process. Recently, special procedures for retrenchment and reallocation have been developed as part of this approach to program planning.
- *Economic incentives*: With the institution viewed as an economic organization, an incentive structure is created that rewards particular types of activities. Each individual faculty member or unit selects programs to be developed on the basis of its response to the existing incentive structure (pp. 306–11).

According to Heydinger, some of the planning styles by virtue of their characteristics foster new programs; other styles are designed primarily to favor the development of existing programs. For example, planning styles that need broad faculty participation are oriented toward maintaining existing programs and result in proposals for only minor program changes: "In the formal democratic style, it is not surprising that as each department reviews its programs, the status quo will emerge as the most widely supported alternative" (Heydinger 1980b, p. 313). Other comprehensive planning styles (e.g., program review, program data, and incremental budgeting) also favor the maintenance of existing programs. In contrast, the program development fund, knowledge development, and entrepreneurial styles foster the growth of new programs by focusing on the individual faculty innovator.

To add to the empirical knowledge of the development of new programs, the author conducted a research survey to explore the extent to which each of Heydinger's planning styles was used in planning new programs. The methodology entailed a two-stage design in which letters were sent to the chief academic officers of 100 four-year colleges and universities (all types). The officers were asked to supply the names and addresses of individuals who were the major "movers and shakers" of successful new programs that had been developed within the last four years. "New program development" was defined as "the process of creating and implementing new academic programs (majors, centers, institutes) that require a significant addition of new funds for people (faculty/staff), capital equipment, new construction, or operating costs." Surveys were sent to 153 individuals, and results were obtained for 110 people (commenting on the introduction of 85 new programs). The programs ranged from a center for theory and simulation with a $7 million operating budget and 75 personnel to a doctoral program in linguistics with three personnel and a $20,000 budget.

The respondents were asked to rate the various planning styles (which were fully described) in terms of the level of influence on their own program's development. The response categories were seven-point scales ranging from "very influential" to "not very influential." Table 5 summarizes the means and modes that were generated for each planning style.

Heydinger noted knowledge development as the most widely used style of academic planning over the centuries. The process is one of developing a course based upon an emerging field of

TABLE 5
PROGRAM PLANNING STYLES

Style	Mean	Mode
Knowledge development	3.5	3
Administrative initiative	3.8	1,7
Entrepreneurial	4.2	1,7
Formal democratic	4.5	7
Curriculum committee	5.0	6
Governing/coordinating board	6.3	7
—		
Problem focused	3.0	2
Program review	3.7	3
Incremental budgeting	4.1	2,7
Economic incentives	4.3	2,7
Needs assessment	4.9	6
Program data	5.2	7
Program development fund	6.0	7

1 = Very influential.
7 = Not very influential.

knowledge. The addition of more courses is followed by the development of a major or a department as the knowledge base expands. Both the mean and the mode suggest that knowledge development is indeed the most influential source of new programs. The entrepreneurial and administrative styles are also prevalent in higher education. But despite the fact that Heydinger suggests that none of the styles exist to the exclusion of the others, it would appear that the hands-off, laissez-faire approach of the faculty entrepreneur conflicts strongly with a style that focuses on the initiative of the administration. In fact, the balanced modes ("very influential" and "not very influential") suggest that these styles are perceived as being mutually exclusive. The formal democratic style is often a function of a more strategic approach to academic planning. Because it requires that all departments (with broad faculty input) periodically draft a plan that highlights the intentions for their academic programs, it is a continuous process. But it should also be noted that the mode is the most extreme "not very influential," probably because this process is well articulated, unlike any of the previous styles. Either it is used or it is not, and apparently at many institutions it is not.

Curriculum committee and governing/coordinating board are also less ambiguous than the initial styles. The curriculum committee is a standing committee organized at the department or college level comprised of faculty, students, and perhaps administrators. But while Heydinger sees this style as being one of the most prevalent in academic planning, these results tend to limit the use of these committees to monitoring program review. Influence of a governing/coordinating board is the newest style; it is obviously one that involves external forces and minimal reliance upon the faculty. Data-based techniques and political pressure are the main sources of program initiative, and so it is unlikely that even if such influences did exist any of the faculty members or administrators in this sample would lend it any credence.

An important observation is that the only external constituency (that could be responsible for initiating or maintaining the process) defined in the "styles" is the governing/coordinating board. And that style has its obvious negative connotations. But the taxonomy as derived does not capture any of the more positive external influences. Perhaps the most significant example of it is a sample of responses to the survey questions, "What is the one most important factor related to the program's success?" and "Why?":

> *A target of opportunity appeared on the horizon at just the moment the administration was ready to hear about it (the catalyst was a letter from a superbly qualified person who wanted a chance to do something with the university). We seized the chance. If we had proposed the idea in the absence of the person, I suspect we'd still be floundering.*

> *Another major factor was the support of professionals (driving force was one individual) who gave us moral support till about 1984. Then they started putting their money where their mouths had been. This was very important money that was leveraged in all sorts of ways (real and psychological) to advance the program.*

Also included in this group of advocates are the various advisory boards or visiting committees that have been set up at

the level of discipline (e.g., an advisory board for a college of business or a school of oceanography). The boards' composition is usually a mix of alumni, scholars, influential laymen, and leaders of the profession. While the purposes of such boards and committees include the promotion of public relations, personnel recruitment, and fund raising, they also can review and evaluate the mission, programs, and services of the college.

By far the most significant style in the "how" category is problem focused. Planning is done as needed—whenever problems or opportunities arise. As such, this orientation matches up well with knowledge development, because the initiative for the new program is diffuse. This report earlier suggested strongly that program review activities do not guarantee program-related decisions; in fact, the tendency is to associate program review with the assessment (and maintenance of the status quo) of ongoing programs. But these results indicate that in many instances the process of program review has been integrated into academic planning. Both the mean and the mode for program review show evidence of substantial influence on the development of new academic programs.

The incremental budgeting style uses the annual budgeting process as the tool for planning academic programs. According to Heydinger's description, "Through the budgeting process, decisions are made on which programs will be developed and which will be cut back. Instead of an independent planning style linked to resource allocation decisions, the determination of the budget is the sole planning tool" (p. 310). As such, this style is more often associated with an institution in a period of constancy or decline. While incremental budgeting seems to be somewhat influential, it is obvious from the nature of the distribution that in most instances incremental budgeting is either "very influential" or "not very influential." No room is available for moderate influence when it comes to its impact on the development of new programs. The same can be said for economic incentives. In some instances—for example, outside funding or a critical need for tuition revenue—the incentive is strong and clear. Usually, however, respondents perceive minimal economic influence.

The final three styles appear not to have much general influence on the innovation of academic programs among those individuals and programs surveyed. Needs assessment, using program development ideas from students, alumni, or potential employers, cannot stand by itself as a viable planning style, but it appears to provide some specific influence in certain circumstances. Of course, while data on needs assessment have intuitive appeal for developing new programs, program data is limited almost exclusively to the monitoring of existing programs. The data do have considerable influence in choices affecting resource allocation in deciding whether to expand a program, but this style, which is usually a function of an office of institutional research, does not have much impact on new programs. And the program development fund is decidedly a style that is either in existence or it is not. Most institutions and new programs in this study were not involved in such funds for innovation. In those few instances where a program development fund was influential, it did have considerable effect, however.

A number of these styles have generated a smattering of research and writings in the higher education literature that are specifically applicable to planning new programs. Interestingly, they all deal with *how* academic planning is done rather than who is responsible for it. These styles include needs assessment, program data, program review, and the program development fund.

Needs assessment
The general interest in needs assessment has been heightened by the fact that "program need" has become a key criterion state and system boards use in the program approval process. As such, a logical question results: Whose needs are of concern? One important category, individual/group clients, refers to persons or groups of persons who are direct clients of the college or university, which would include students, alumni, faculty, and staff. Another category, interest-based communities, refers to large groups identified as entities working toward a well-defined interest or mission, for example, government communities, private corporations, and local communities. A second question then results: What types of needs are of concern? They could include economic outcomes, outcomes related to human characteristics (aspirations, competencies and skills, and so on), specialized knowledge and understanding, and outcomes related to resources and services (Lenning et al. 1977, p. 27). Further, various mechanisms are available to measure needs: survey methods, open-ended interviews, data about complaints, among others.

Much of the literature on assessment deals with ongoing programs, and another large portion is concerned with external constituencies, such as corporations (covered later). A small amount of literature, however, concerns needs assessment of students.

Exit interviews with students dropping out of department programs can provide useful information about student perceptions of department strengths and weaknesses. The findings may relate to specific instructors as well as to curriculum offerings. Similar information can be secured from graduates of the department. In both cases the results can be put to good, immediate use in aligning the department more closely to appropriate and legitimate student interests. Information gathered in this fashion, together with that gleaned from developments in the discipline and needs of the surrounding community, may also suggest the importance of developing some new curricular thrusts (Bennett 1983, p. 54).

While the development of instruments to gather such information is largely specific to an institution, a number of student survey instruments have been developed (e.g., Denney, Conrath, and Stiff 1979). Further, a series of questionnaires developed by the College Board and the National Center for Higher Education Management Systems are targeted toward entering students, continuing students, former students, program-completed/graduating students, and recent alumni (Cherin and Armijo 1980).

Program data

Another planning style that has received some attention is the use of internally generated data to assess a program's strengths and capabilities. The use and improvement of a management information system have become indispensable steps in making the kind of strategic choices that need to be made when facing tough choices in a no-growth environment (Keller 1983, p. 131). In one case example of using institutional data to plan academic programs, the authors use the development of a unified evaluation, budgeting, and planning system at Michigan State University to show how a quantitative assessment of all academic units enabled administrators to compare programs across an array of common variables (Freeman and Simpson 1980). "At last they had, in a single compact package, information about their unit and how it compared to various college and university averages . . . data that could be used to determine how the department was functioning, to indicate what had to be improved, and very importantly, to support their budget request" (p. 30). Such hard comparative data, when combined with other subjective data, provide strong support for decisions about allocating resources. And such decisions, under conditions of fiscal restraint, are the critical mechanisms for generating the institutional flexibility required to ensure that innovative program ideas are not starved. More generally, a number of data-driven planning tools can be useful in the development of new programs. These tools help organize data that emanate from such offices as the registrar, admissions, and academic affairs. One such tool, for example, is the Induced Course Load Matrix, which provides information on such items as interaction of curricula and projections for and patterns of enrollment (Kieft, Armijo, and Bucklew 1978, p. 28).

Any assessment of program strengths and capabilities that results in "building" strategies may signal the development of related new programs.

Program review

In the same manner as program data, program review focuses on existing programs. But the development of new academic programs has become increasingly a function of a strategic planning process. The use of portfolio analysis as an evaluation tool has received some attention as a means for identifying the strengths of ongoing programs (Kotler and Murphy 1981, pp. 481–83). Instead of using market share and market growth as the axes on the matrix, however, an adaptation to academic programs might use the dimensions of "centrality to the institutional mission" and "quality level of programs" (see table 6). The table also identifies a third dimension, "market viability," shown in parentheses.

The measures of these three dimensions come from different sources. Measures of quality can come from outside experts, measures of outcome (employment), reputational ratings, accreditation, or individual program reviews (Shirley and Volkwein 1978, p. 476). Measures of centrality must necessarily come from institutional administrators, measures of market viability from information collected from analyses of the environment. The resulting strategies identified—build, hold, reduce, or terminate—have specific applications to the development of new academic programs. Reduction or termination strategies are important because they have the potential to free up resources to be used to fund innovative new programs. More im-

TABLE 6
ACADEMIC PORTFOLIO EVALUATION TOOL

	Centrality		
Quality	*High*	*Medium*	*Low*
High	Psychology (MV-H)* Decision: –Build size –Build quality		Home Economics (MV-H) Decision: –Build size –Hold quality
Medium		Geography (MV-M) Decision: –Hold size –Hold quality	
Low	Philosophy (MV-L) Decision: –Reduce size –Build quality		Classical Languages (MV-L) Decision: –Reduce size or terminate

*(MV-H, -M, -L) = Market Value–High, Medium, or Low.

Source: Kotler and Murphy 1981, p. 482.

portant, however, any assessment of program strengths and capabilities that results in "building" strategies may signal the development of related new programs.

Program development fund
The Carnegie Council's *Three Thousand Futures* (1980) includes a checklist of imperatives for colleges and universities for meeting the problems through the end of this century. It includes the following item:

> ***Encourage Innovation and Flexibility.*** *Develop curriculum that is sensitive to change but also to emphasis on general education. Establish fund for innovation. Avoid too high a proportion of tenured-in faculty. Encourage new programs and instructional techniques* (p. 130).

Several case examples illustrate how such innovation or program development funds operate. First, the University of Michigan's Priority Fund was established to respond to changing interests and opportunities and to provide greater support for existing programs of high priority (Mims 1980). Reducing each unit's base budget by an amount equal to 1 percent of the previous year's budget generated a pool of $1.5 million. Then, several criteria (e.g., centrality, future societal demands, anticipated enrollment) were applied to proposals. New York University's Curricular Development Fund has aided in the creation of over 100 new programs and courses (Oliva 1986). Over its lifetime (conceived in 1977), the fund has shifted its focus as needs have shifted. Two of its six different purposes are to examine new programs designed to attract new audiences and to permit reorganization or redevelopment of current programs and courses to meet current needs. The new programs are wide-ranging: the program in social welfare, the creative writing program, the medieval and Renaissance studies program, the center for Latin American and Caribbean studies, and the NYU summer musical theatre workshop. Oklahoma State University's Excellence Fund was created by taxing educational and general budgets of major areas and units by an amount equivalent to up to 6 percent of a baseline year (Mims 1980). The resulting fund was then used to support new and existing programs that would bring national attention and recognition to the university in selected areas. In this case, six criteria were used to evaluate programs and establish priorities: centrality to the university's mission, productivity, demand, resources used, vitality, and distinctiveness.

The key considerations involved in this approach are adequate funding, a commitment to change, and new ventures backed up by an actual dollar investment:

Colleges talk a lot about developing new ideas and information. But it is startling how few actually set aside money for promising new ventures. One way to find out quickly if a university means what it says about its creativity and pushing out the frontiers of knowledge is to ask how much of its budget is set aside annually as risk capital to sponsor new ventures. Every really good college and serious university should have a venture capital fund (Keller 1983, p. 168).

Colleges and universities do not take seriously the relationship between internal strengths and capabilities and new program development. Consequently, program planning priorities are not made on the basis of comprehensive, strategic information. Each function tends to proceed in parallel—various evaluation activities (program review, accreditation self-studies, for example) on the one hand and new program choices on the other. Most internal assessment projects, therefore, remain descriptive, burdensome, mechanical efforts that are largely unrelated to opportunities for new programs. In effect, such important introspection is isolated from the difficult but necessary process of setting priorities.

External Needs and Opportunities

As noted earlier, one of the basic characteristics of strategic planning is that it places great emphasis on the conditions of the environment, seeking to match institutional capabilities with environmental conditions to achieve goals. In fact, "The first step in strategic planning is to analyze the environment in which the organization operates, trying to identify the leading trends and their implications for the organization" (Kotler 1982, p. 44). More specifically, the role of environmental assessment in strategic planning is to identify environmental factors relevant to the mission of the organization; to assess favorable or unfavorable impacts of events, conditions, and trends on priorities; to develop scenarios; and to devise realistic strategies for creating viable futures for the organization (Glover and Holmes 1983, p. 7).

A college or university must ask itself several questions in conducting an environmental analysis: (1) What are the major trends in the environment? (2) What are the implications of those trends for the organization? and (3) What are the most significant opportunities and threats? One attempt to provide a strategic framework for thinking about the external environment and its opportunities is shown in table 7. This matrix of opportunities is a broadly based mechanism enabling colleges and universities to imagine new "product" options systematically. And one such product option involves the development of new programs. The matrix suggests that different strategies apply to products—in this case academic programs—depending upon the nature of the markets—that is, external opportunities.

At least one author has looked at the notion of "new markets" in terms of recruiting new students and has developed eight principles to govern the creation of new programs for new student markets (to maintain enrollments and generate needed revenues): (1) programs must lead to a credential, degree, or certificate that has a positive relationship to an individual's

TABLE 7
PRODUCT/MARKET OPPORTUNITY STRATEGY

Markets	Existing	Products Modified	New
Existing	1. Market Penetration	4. Product Modification	7. Production Innovation
		−Short courses −Evening program −Weekend program −New delivery system	−New courses −New departments −New schools
Geographical	2. Geographical Expansion −New areas of city −New cities −Foreign	5. Modification for Dispersed Markets −Programs offered on military bases or at U.S. firms abroad	8. Geographic Innovation
New	3. New Markets −Individual •Senior Citizens •Homemakers •Ethnic minorites −Institutional •Business firms •Social agencies	6. Modification for New Markets −Individual •Senior citizens −Institutional •Business •Government	9. Total Innovation −New courses −New departments −New schools

Source: Kotler and Murphy 1981, p. 484.

present and future income; (2) programs should be such that students can obtain tuition and fees through various aid programs or from employers; (3) programs should be effectively taught at times convenient to substantial numbers of students, by faculty paid at rates less than those paid regular full-time faculty, and using relatively inexpensive modes of instruction; (4) programs should be in a field in which a real shortage of credentialed individuals exists; (5) programs should not require specialized teaching space, such as laboratories or clinical facilities; (6) programs should ideally lead directly to an acceptable credential or license, without validation by any other agency; (7) programs should be in a reasonably stable field so that outlines and materials can be prepared relatively easily and inexpensively with the expectation that they will not become quickly dated; and (8) programs should be such that they can be taught by any number of individuals generally acquainted with a field (Mayhew 1979, pp. 179–82).

While a consistent literature has developed (e.g., Cope 1981; Glover and Holmes 1983) that details the relevance of an active and ongoing assessment of the external environment, mechanisms for gathering the necessary data to decide which specific programs and which markets have not been well defined. The notion of "environmental scanning," a set of techniques for monitoring trends, has been advocated as a college or university's radar system; scanning enables decision makers to detect changes ahead and to adjust course (Clugston 1986, p. 3). The scanning process has been described as having four specific aspects: (1) selecting information resources to scan, (2) searching or screening for information resources, (3) identifying criteria by which to scan, and (4) determining special action for the scanning results (Renfro and Morrison 1983, p. 22). In addition to the general literature on environmental scanning in higher education, some specific attention has been paid to two organizational units as scanning agents—the office of institutional research and a futures committee. The institutional research office can be especially valuable in pulling together various studies and statistics to support an external assessment (Glover and Holmes 1983), and the appointment of a futures committee using such techniques as probability-impact charts and futures wheels can give the institution useful data on trends (Morrison 1985).

The specific relationship between the external environment and program development has received little attention in the literature on higher education. Perhaps the only specific discussion of this link is offered in a review of the major factors that influence academic program priorities (Shirley and Volkwein 1978). The external influences include:

- *The social/demographic characteristics of the geographical area*

- *Location in the area of unique institutions or organizations*
- *The types of industry located in the area*
- *The existence of other educational institutions, their missions, and the opportunities for collaboration*
- *Other distinguishing characteristics or resources of the geographical area that may present unique opportunities*
- *Distinguishing characteristics of the area that constrain the institution's ability to develop certain areas of knowledge* (p. 475).

The assessment of such external considerations reveals what a college or university might do or, in some instances, what it should do. For example, "assume that the environmental assessment concludes that a particular industry constitutes a definite technological resource for the fulfillment of an educational mission . . . . What new programs could be developed to capitalize on this resource?" (p. 476). Other writers have briefly discussed the use of advisory boards (Lynton 1982) and surveys of community needs (Lee and Gilmour 1977) to generate information on the needs and wants of external constituencies.

A number of descriptive case studies and almost-anecdotal accounts of newly developed programs can be arranged into various categories. These external forces are grouped accordingly: state, federal, and foundation; corporate; other colleges and universities; and social issues.

State, federal, and foundation
One obvious force that is beginning to have some impact on innovative programming ideas is the expanded role that colleges and universities are having in the economic development of their states and regions. A recent survey of 11 major state-supported universities noted that institutions have numerous opportunities to enhance the economic future of their states (Smith, Drabenstott, and Gibson 1987), ranging from extension service in land-grant institutions to numerous joint state/corporate/university research endeavors. Academic programs, however, are another story:

In spite of the recent attention being given to the universities' role in economic development, few of the universities have formed an economic development agenda with clearly stated objectives. Few major changes have been made in university programs to reflect economic development efforts, and few resources have been earmarked for economic development (p. 11).

Smith, Drabenstott, and Gibson cite two examples of new academic programs: At Kansas State University, undergraduate teaching and basic research in material sciences, biotechnology (plant genetics), value-added agricultural products, and industrial technology transfer (including robotics) are the major focuses of a new emphasis on economic development, and the Columbia campus of the University of Missouri boasts two state-funded programs to build centers of academic and research excellence—a molecular biology program and a food for the 21st century program (p. 12). Perhaps the best example of a directed effort by a state to link colleges and universities to the state's economic future is in New Jersey. The New Jersey Department of Higher Education offers competitive grants to finance innovative programs in computer science, the humanities, mathematics, and sciences at both public and private institutions. Further, the recently formed 16-member New Jersey Commission on Science and Technology has identified certain fields—among them industrial ceramics, biotechnology, and hazardous-waste management—as potential growth industries for the state (Mooney 1987).

A few national sources of grants have programs designed to support academic program initiatives. For example, many of the women's studies programs (for example, at Yale and at Old Dominion University) have their roots in pilot grants from the National Endowment for the Humanities (Brown 1984). New programs, centers, and institutes have been added to colleges and universities simply because a foundation has indicated a willingness to support efforts in a specific area. From 1970 to 1976, for example, private foundations gave over $13 million (218 grants) to higher education institutions to support funding for women's programs. While much of this funding went to research and scholarships, almost $2 million went directly to "educational materials and programs." Major private agencies like the Ford Foundation, the Carnegie Corporation, the Mellon Foundation, and the Rockefeller Foundation were the most active. The extent of foundations' efforts to support new programming vis-à-vis research, scholarships, or other types of activities has not been addressed in the literature on higher education, however.

Corporate

A 1982 article on corporate education made the following observation:

> *Every observer agrees on one fundamental issue: Academic institutions must learn to work together with industry in defining educational needs and developing appropriate content and format. Although in recent years there has been some movement toward real cooperation, the prevalent mode continues to be that a group of faculty in splendid isolation identifies what it believes to be an external need, designs what it considers to be the best way of meeting it—and then tries to interest individual as well as corporate clients. That simply does not work and is resented as an example of academic arrogance* (Lynton 1982, p. 44).

Two years later, another survey offered direct evidence of the extent of academe's involvement in collaborative activities with business (El-Khawas 1985). The most prevalent link was through advisory panels, followed by equipment grants and scholarship/loan programs. Farther down the list was a smaller yet growing set of activities involving joint programs. Specifically, 19 percent of the colleges and universities in the sample reported that they had degree programs that were "jointly developed and sponsored with corporations." These innovations were found primarily among community colleges and public doctoral institutions.

Perhaps the links that have received the most attention in the literature on higher education are those involving allied health programs and, more recently, executive MBA programs. Hospital-university relations have grown rapidly over the last two decades. Unlike the many educational programs that are solely campus based, programs that educate health manpower have reached beyond the college or university for sponsorship or for affiliated relationships that provide sites for clinical training. A 1984 review found 8,000 college-based, allied health programs in areas like audiology, dietetics, nuclear medicine technology, respiratory therapy, and sonography (McFadden and Cohen 1984, p. 54). The executive MBA program has been a more recent phenomenon. It is an academic program offered on a flexible time schedule that enables middle or senior management executives to acquire new skills in such areas as computer information systems, international business, strategic planning, and entrepreneurship. Many, if not most, of the students are sponsored by their corporations. One recent survey found that while only 10 institutions offered such programs a decade ago, more than 100 programs were currently in place, with new ones being developed (Van Doren, Smith, and Biglin 1986): "The Executive MBA has become a major force in business education, a revenue source for universities, and a university-business connection that promotes corporate financial and human resource contributions" (p. 34).

Again, it must be mentioned that community colleges and comprehensive colleges appear to have been particularly adept at generating specific mechanisms for translating occupational needs into academic programs (see, for example, Abrams et al. 1983, Maxwell and West 1980, and Long 1983).

Other colleges and universities

Interinstitutional cooperation has become increasingly popular among colleges and universities as a viable planning strategy to improve the development of academic programs. While formal relationships, such as those between institutions under a single state coordinating agency, are covered later in this section, other types of interinstitutional relationships include sharing data informally and consortia. A number of different cooperative approaches have been developed and implemented: articulation agreements, student and staff exchange programs, resource sharing agreements, educational exchange programs, private/public cooperative agreements, and international exchange programs (Miller 1986).

Perhaps the most topical example of this type of program development is the Holmes Group initiative in the area of teacher education. The members of the group, approximately 90 institutions, including many state research universities, have generated the Holmes Group Report. The report contains seven major assertions and numbers of key recommendations concerning the reform of teacher education. For example:

Create a five-year program. The current, more or less traditional, four-year teacher education program is mediocre and structurally and conceptually unsound. Therefore, it ought to be scrapped and replaced with a five-year integrated pro-

gram. In short, the Holmes Group Report suggests taps for the undergraduate teacher education program, whether in small colleges or large universities (Magrath 1986, p. 8).

In such a way, some new program features may be the result of a collaborative effort among a group of institutions, with the program specifics determined by needs at individual campuses.

Social issues

New programs may also be the result of external pressures conjoined with internal interests. Both women's studies and black studies are examples of programs that resulted from a shift in social patterns that also had an evolving internal advocacy (Dressel 1987, p. 105). Women's studies programs are well documented in the literature. The "women's movement," supported by various granting agencies and advocated by a core group of professors and administrators, created the necessary critical mass. Curriculum development grew slowly at first, but as of 1984 over 500 women's studies programs existed in colleges and universities (Brown 1984).

While colleges and universities have begun to look outward, it is evident that the extent of this new perspective has been largely a function of the type of institution and the nature of that institution's activities. Certain types of institutions are better at looking outward. Research universities are overwhelmingly discipline driven. Professors and administrators in such institutions place their research interests above all other university functions. In contrast, professors and administrators in community colleges and comprehensive colleges are primarily interested in teaching and satisfying consumer-driven needs. In this sense, "research universities are inner-directed, guided by a multitude of disciplinary directives. Direct-service colleges are other-directed, much more dependent on the meeting of consumer wishes" (M. Clark 1983, p. 110). It would appear that many institutions are just now attempting to find the proper balance, that is, developing a service orientation that looks for outside relationships that go beyond the advisory role while still encouraging internally generated entrepreneurship and maintaining responsibility for the quality and standards of its academic programs.

Program and Priority Decisions

While no set approach exists to making program and priority decisions, it is apparent that the three essential inputs are mis-

While no set approach exists to making program and priority decisions, it is apparent that the three essential inputs are mission, internal factors, and external factors.

sion, internal factors, and external factors. The resulting "match" based upon objective data (e.g., estimates of budget and demand) and subjective data (e.g., institutional mission) is pursued within generalized decision-making processes (e.g., collegial, political, rational, bureaucratic, anarchical). Only one concerted effort has been made to describe various aspects of this "match" (Barak 1982), which offers a number of general conclusions:

- At nearly every public college or university, a series of formal internal processes and procedures is required to obtain program approval.
- Formal procedures are being increasingly used in independent four-year liberal arts colleges and private junior colleges.
- Reasons cited for conducting approvals include (in order of importance) a desire "to determine if documented needs justify the program," a need "to determine if resources [are] sufficient to support a quality program," and a desire "to determine if the program is consistent with institutional role and mission."
- An additional reason that seems to be more important now than in the past is that careful scrutiny on campus acts "as a control against the inclination at the state level to select programs for funding in a more political way" (pp. 15–24).

Additional specific findings include the observation that the individuals who take part in the program approval and the extent of their involvement are generally in accord with institutional structure. That is, those persons most highly involved in new program approval (in rank order) included the faculty proposing the program, the college dean, the department chair/head, the academic vice president, other faculty (same institution), consultants (program related), trustees, students, a state agency, consultants (general), and the system staff.

The specific nature of the procedures involved depends to a great extent on the institution. Formality and size, however, do seem to be related: Larger institutions tend to have more formal processes. The criteria used in decision making fall into four general categories: need for program, costs and benefits of the program, objectives of the program, and accrediting requirements. Within the category of "need," six items are defined, with justification ranked first, followed by students' interests and job opportunities. Within the category of "cost and benefits," the 12 items on the list are headed by projected enrollment, needed physical facilities, sources of funding, projected graduates, and quality of faculty.

One area of Barak's study that deserves special attention is the differentiation between the decision practices of community colleges and other institutions of higher education. Perhaps the foremost distinction is the community colleges' heavy reliance on criteria covering "need for the program." These criteria emphasize manpower studies, that is, employment prospects. More traditional colleges and universities emphasize students' interests and enrollment projections, that is, input variables. Additionally, a great deal more research has been conducted among various agencies and institutes affiliated with community colleges regarding assessment and decision-making tools. For example, the Cornell Institute for Research and Development in Occupational Education has compiled an exhaustive procedural checklist and guide (Beilby and Corwin 1976). The planning/decision system includes seven sections, which are subdivided into major topic areas, topics, and subtopics:

1. *Identity:* What would be the general content of the program?
2. *Articulation:* Does the program fit college, local, regional, and state plans?
3. *Resources:* Does the college have the resources to conduct the program?
4. *Students:* How many and what kinds of students will the program attract?
5. *Employment:* Will the graduates of the program be able to obtain jobs commensurate with their training?
6. *Support:* Will the program be supported within the college and the community?
7. *Evaluation:* How will the program be evaluated?

Another distinction noted in Barak's analysis is that many more community colleges use staff offices (e.g., the director of planning and development) to support gathering the information. In four-year colleges and universities, program proposals are overwhelmingly initiated by faculty, but at two-year institutions, the faculty is just one of many sources.

In addition to these broadly based materials on program decisions and priorities, at least two specific considerations are mentioned in the literature. First, given fiscal constraints, institutional leaders do not have the discretion to approve all expansions of programs and proposals for new programs. It is therefore crucial that decision makers be devoted to a "selective strategy" (Balderston 1981, p. 58). The selective strategy must be supported by two other strategies—a "comparative strategy" and an "integrative strategy." The choice of program alternatives must be based upon the notion of *optimal use of available resources*. And any judgment of what is optimal must be made on a comparison of costs and benefits between one program and other possible programs (Ohio Board 1973, p. 23). Finally, academic and facilities planning and budgeting must be carefully integrated to translate informed choices into the effective implementation of a new program (Tack, Rentz, and Russell 1984, p. 8).

Program Approval at the System and State Levels
Various types of system and state boards were created during the 1950s and 1960s as mechanisms to assist the orderly growth of higher education. Currently, all states have some form of statewide postsecondary governing, coordinating, or planning board or agency. Most fall in one of two categories: a governing board with regulatory powers involved in budget management and the operational policies of the institutions under their governance, or a coordinating board with limited legal responsibility for institutional management and operation but charged with responsibility for the diffusion of information (Millett 1984, pp. 99–102). The remaining states, perhaps 10 or so, have some sort of advisory board or a mixed arrangement. In virtually all cases, however, these agencies and boards have at least some role in the development and approval of new programs.

Historically, the involvement of these agencies and boards in the development of new academic programs has been viewed as a positive force. As a means to coordinate planning, academic departments are competent to decide the proper structure and content of a program or curriculum, while governing boards and administrative officers can best decide how those programs relate to a particular institution's role. It remains, however, for the central coordinating or governing agency to apply its judgment as to how a proposed program relates to the programs of other institutions in the state. The concern for unnecessary duplication, in the face of rapid expansion over the last several decades, has minimized the tendency to proliferate programs without regard to what others are doing.

The process of review may include any or all of a series of steps:

1. A number of states require prior notification or approval of planning for a new program. This step may be as informal as a phone call or letter of intent, but it is designed to avoid duplicative planning and to encourage cooperation and communication before formal procedures are initiated.
2. To ensure the program has been thoroughly reviewed by the institution, most boards require a statement of approval by the institution, either its governing board or its chief executive.
3. Most states use a prescribed format for submission of programs to ensure some degree of comparability among requests.
4. A number of states currently require an interinstitutional review, which may consist of having each similar institution in the state comment on the proposal or review by a formal interinstitutional committee.
5. Some states, in addition to or in place of interinstitutional review, engage in a process of outside review, which may be done by formal or informal committees of out-of-state consultants chosen by the board's staff or the institution or both.
6. Each of these steps may be, and usually is, followed by the board staff's review or by a review by a committee of the board (Millard 1980, p. 90).

A review of policies and procedures regarding program approval at the system or state level describes a number of trends (Barak 1982). First, responsibilities for program approval are still growing, and "clearly, the final determination for new program proposals has shifted out of the hands of the institutions and into the state-level postsecondary agencies" (p. 27). Second, the scope of programs under review has broadened considerably to include both majors and minors as well as concentrations. Third, agencies are now using multiple criteria and requiring more exact answers. Fourth, several states now ask for measures of a program's performance to check up on programs after the initial approval. Fifth, a number of state agencies now require (either formally or informally) some form of "start one–stop one" approach to approval of new programs. And finally, more states are using a planning rather than an incremental approach requiring that "new program proposals be coordinated with an overall planning effort, generally as part of the state's master-planning process" (p. 31).

Given the evolving nature of the policies and procedures of system and state agencies in this area, the author conducted a comprehensive review of 42 such regulations in early 1988. An initial observation is that regulations governing program approval are indeed being changed. Almost two-thirds of the policies and procedures regarding program approval have been revised within the last four years. The major shifts in policy have occurred in the areas of preproposal and postapproval, reallocation, scope, planning, and criteria.

Preproposal and postapproval

More than half of the governing or coordinating boards have now incorporated a preliminary stage before a proposal is submitted. The agency, title, description, and lead times (the minimum time between submission of the "request to plan" and the submission of a formal proposal for a new program) for seven examples are detailed in table 8. The obvious intent of these preproposal exercises is to give state and system staff members a peek into each institution's mind. In addition to avoiding duplicative planning, such exercises may also be useful in sparing institutions the embarrassment of a formal rejection later on (Berdahl 1971, p. 159).

While the trend toward postapproval performance measures is still not widespread, a number of specific examples of this phenomenon can be described. As part of a program proposal, for instance, Connecticut requires institutions to define "procedures and criteria for the ongoing evaluation of the program design and delivery system." Similarly, Maryland asks institutions to "describe the specific methods that will be used for evaluation of the proposed program following implementation." Other states and systems (e.g., New Mexico and Wisconsin) have a mandatory review period in which data about enrollments must be submitted to the agency. And, finally, several states and systems (e.g., Connecticut and Louisiana) give only limited approvals to a proposal for a new program. The Louisiana Board of Regents grants conditional approval:

All degree programs—associate, certificate, baccalaureate,

TABLE 8
PREPROPOSAL REQUESTS

System	Title, Components, and Lead time
Florida	The Request for Authorization to Study Feasibility of a New Degree Program includes a section on whatever steps have already been taken to explore the appropriateness of the program, a statistical section (e.g., manpower, census data), a timetable, and a budget (four months).*
Kentucky	The Program Advisory Statement includes a brief description, its degree level, current status within the institution, source of funding, and likely submission date (August 1 and February 1).
Louisiana	The Letter of Intent includes the title, a brief description of the purpose of the projected program, and demonstration that the program would be within the scope of the institution, complement existing programs, avoid unnecessary duplication, supply present and future needed manpower, and be within the institution's anticipated resources (one year).
Maryland	The Prospectus includes the title, rationale for initiating the action, appropriateness to mission, proposed implementation date, source of students, impact on facilities, and estimated costs associated with the proposed program during the next five years (one month).
New Jersey	The Preliminary Program Announcement includes name and degree proposed, site, objectives, relationship to institutional and state master plans, similarity to other programs, demand, and date to be offered (21 days).
South Carolina	The Letter of Intent (one page total) includes a brief description of the purpose and justification for the program, the estimated implementation date, and a preliminary estimate of additional resources required (six months).
Wisconsin	The Entitlement to Plan includes a brief description of the program and an ordered list (with rationale) of all programs within a four-year planning cycle (updated annually).

*Lead times shown in parentheses.

masters, specialist, doctorate—[that] the Board of Regents deems worthy of implementation shall initially be given "conditional approval." After the program has been in operation for four . . . years, or after the program graduates its first class, whichever occurs first, a review of the program by the submitting institution will be required by the Board. The reviews shall include the following information:

  1. Demonstration that requirements of quality education are met in the program.
  2. Evidence that the submitted need is met by the program.
  3. Evidence that the program has served the number of students projected in the original application.

If the first review of the program is unsatisfactory, the program will either be discontinued or a second review will be required. Should a second review prove unsatisfactory to the Board, conditional approval will be withdrawn and the program terminated. A satisfactory review will lead to approval of the program.

What is clearly evident is that the period for a decision regarding planning for new programs is being extended at the state and system levels. A "yes" or "no" vote on a proposal for a program is being replaced in many states by a series of conditional votes.

Requirements for reallocation

While an increasing amount of literature is available on the strategies (e.g., reallocation) related to organizations in a state of constancy or decline, concern about this topic for system-level and state-level higher education programs is also increasing. For example, a discussion of important state-level issues suggests that administrators will be expected to show that education institutions can change—and in ways other than by incremental growth—and concludes that the public will support new programs only after the institution has demonstrated that it has exhausted the possibilities of internal reallocation (Magrath 1980, p. 71). The "start one–stop one" approach to the approval of new programs that requires institutions to terminate a program each time a new program is proposed is one extreme way to win public support (Barak 1982).

The fact remains, however, that most agencies do not specifically refer to "reallocation" in their policies and procedures. A number of states (Indiana, Nevada, South Dakota, and Virginia, for example) request information on the reallocation of existing resources as a possible source of funds in the "costs" section of the proposal. Almost one-third of the states refer in some way to the "possibility" of using some source of reallo-cation to help with the costs of the new program. The Colorado Commission on Higher Education asks one of the most direct set of questions: Will any program be deemphasized with the approval of this program? How has the governing board dealt with or how will it deal with issues regarding the allocation of resources?

Scope

It is certainly possible to confirm the observation that the scope of reviews of new academic programs has been extended in re-cent years (Barak 1982). In fact, the scope has been extended in two directions. First, as coordinating boards have extended their responsibilities through legislative actions, technical and trade schools, community colleges, and private colleges and universities have become subject to statewide review. The Min-nesota Higher Education Coordinating Board, for example, op-erates under the following legislative authorization:

> *The legislature has authorized the Board to do the following: review, approve or disapprove, make recommendations, and identify priorities with respect to all plans and proposals for new or additional programs of instruction or substantial changes in existing programs to be established in or offered by the University of Minnesota, the state universities, the community colleges, and public area vocational-technical in-stitutes and private collegiate and noncollegiate institutions offering postsecondary education . . . .*

In addition, the scope of the review has been extended within many institutions to include not only all degree pro-grams but also minors, concentrations, and off-campus pro-grams. Those programs proposed to have their requirements or curricular components significantly altered are also in many cases obliged to undergo review—a drastic change when one considers that even within the last decade, many state agencies reviewed only major graduate programs involving requests for new funding.

Planning

The previous section reviewed the literature on strategic plan-ning as it relates to program review, program discontinuance, and development of new programs. In the recent past, many statewide boards and agencies of higher education engaged in long-range planning in the form of master planning (Millard 1980, p. 79). A rolling, or continuous, planning process, involving a series of different planning processes, has been a more recent trend commensurate with a volatile environment. This method involves two basic approaches to state-level program approval: planning and/or budgeting, and incremental (Barak 1982, p. 31). The planning and/or budgeting approach requires the institution to show that the new program meets the requirements of the state's master plan *before* it is considered for approval, while the incremental, one-at-a-time approach involves institutions' submitting proposals at their own convenience.

A review of 1988 policies and procedures yields a mixed bag of relationships between different approaches to planning and proposals for new programs. In most states, the agencies involved rely on a straightforward list of criteria to judge the appropriateness of a proposed program, and state or institutional master (or strategic) planning is not overtly mentioned. But a smattering of references to planning are incorporated into some policies and procedures. For example, Nevada's new format for proposals requires the institution to describe the relationship of the program's objectives to the "campus master plan," and New Jersey requires the institution to address the relationship between the new program proposed and the "institutional and state master plans" in its preliminary program announcement. Other coordinating boards (e.g., Tennessee and Colorado) also explicitly refer to institutional or state planning. Perhaps the most extensive effort at detailing the relationship between developing and planning new academic programs is the recently adopted (November 1987) *Policies and Procedures for Six-Year Curricular Plans* by the State Council of Higher Education for Virginia. The council, which is charged by statute with the responsibility of reviewing and approving or disapproving all new academic programs proposed by any public institution of higher education, has developed a set of policies and procedures to provide a systematic framework within which new academic programs can be planned and initiated:

Every two years, the Council of Higher Education requests each state-supported institution to bring up to date its six-year curricular plan and to submit it to the Council for review and approval. Long-range curricular plans for all insti-

tutions will enable the Council to evaluate requests for new academic programs within the total context of higher education in the Commonwealth and to plan systemwide development of higher education in a coherent fashion.

Finally, some implicit movement toward a planning orientation is apparent. Numbers of agencies have begun to define specific time periods for their acceptance of proposed new programs. Many of these time periods are linked to budget cycles and consequently may result in a planning orientation based upon concerns about resources.

Evaluative criteria

The appropriateness of new programs must ultimately be judged on the basis of information regarding various objective measures and subjective intuitions. Obviously, the specific items that are used in the analyses largely depend on the system and institutions involved. A large state research university should not have its program proposals judged in the same manner as a small private liberal arts college. Descriptions of general categories exist in the literature. For example, one author suggests three major criteria for judging the new programs proposed by state-funded institutions: institutional readiness, the state's need, and the state's ability to finance the proposal (Berdahl 1971, pp. 161–63). In this case, institutional readiness covers a range of items, including the adequacy of institutional faculty, facilities, and library resources. In terms of the state's need, a distinction is made between a state's *need* for a program and students' *demand* for it. A particular state, for example, may have more requests for a doctorate in education than for one in mathematics, yet the state's need may be far greater for highly trained mathematicians. And in judging need, regional and even national (as well as state) factors should be considered. Finally, while duplication is a concern, only *unnecessary* duplication is the issue. In some instances, perhaps where demand and needs are exceedingly strong, a certain amount of legitimate overlap occurs. The state's ability to finance the proposal is included in this categorization, because regardless of need and institutional ability, it does not always follow that expending the state's funds for the program represents the best investment of scarce resources.

Another review of evaluative criteria found that the items used to judge proposed new programs included several different

One author suggests three major criteria for judging the new programs proposed by state-funded institutions: institutional readiness, the state's need, and the state's ability to finance the proposed.

TABLE 9

A COMPOSITE OF EVALUATIVE CRITERIA FOR NEW ACADEMIC PROGRAMS

Description and objectives
1. Title of program
2. Degree or certificate awarded
3. Curriculum outline/sample
4. Skills acquired
5. Requirements for degree
6. Requirements for admission
7. Limitations on enrollment
8. New or reorganized academic unit
9. Department or school responsible
10. New courses versus existing courses
11. HEGIS and CIP program codes
12. Program objectives
13. Measures of program's performance
14. Program faculty, administrators

Mission
1. Compatibility with master plan
2. Institutional compatibility
3. Relationship to curricular changes
4. Ability to build on institution's strengths

Accreditation and licensure
1. Existing accreditation agencies
2. Requirements for eligibility
3. Planning for accreditation
4. Special resources required
5. Initial costs of accreditation
6. Subsequent annual costs

Duplication
1. Similar programs offered
2. Justification for overlap
3. Possibilities for cooperative programs
4. Facilities, faculty cooperation

varieties: purposes and objectives, needs analysis, cost analysis, resource analysis, program accreditation, and availability of adequate student financial aid (Barak and Berdahl 1977, p. 26.) Table 9 presents a composite of the categories and specific items present in policies and procedures for new programs.

Systems' and states' involvement in the development of new programs has increased dramatically within the last decade. As such, agencies are asking more difficult questions using multiple criteria, time frames have lengthened considerably, and the definition of "new program" has broadened. While much of this increased activity is necessary, this more comprehensive approach is becoming "too lengthy and inflexible" (Barak 1982, p. 31). Several observations can be made regarding this

TABLE 9 (*continued*)

A COMPOSITE OF EVALUATIVE CRITERIA FOR NEW ACADEMIC PROGRAMS

Needs
1. Opportunities for employment
2. Industry and government interests
3. Historical and projected job trends
4. Impact on economic development

Students
1. Projected enrollments
2. Source of students
3. Enrollments for similar programs
4. Projections for graduation
5. Special preparation needed
6. Sources of financial support
7. Students' characteristics
8. Requirements for transferability

Requirements for resources
1. Current or new faculty
2. Expenses to recruit faculty
3. Library holdings
4. Capital equipment
5. Operating expenses
6. Resources for support
7. Internship or clinical sites
8. Needs for facilities and space

Financing
1. Start-up appropriations
2. Federal or other grant funds
3. Reallocation
4. Detailed five-year budgets

explosion of information. For example, the nature of the information and how it is handled are quite different, depending upon whether the agency is a coordinating or a governing board. The diffusion of information is especially important to coordinating boards, as they lack significant authoritative mandate to compel certain behaviors. As such, an orientation toward sharing information appears to be greater; for example, the New Mexico Commission on Higher Education has a section called "information requirements" in its policies and procedures. The section is divided into two parts, one of which contains information (e.g., specific characteristics of other programs offered at New Mexico institutions and national statistics) generated by the commission. Governing boards, in contrast, tend to set standards and require informational analyses. The Kansas Board of Regents, for example, states that a proposed program "will not be considered sound unless" the program can hit program targets regarding demand, library resources, lower-level graduation rates, and instructional staff (e.g., doctoral programs require eight Ph.D.s on the staff, master's programs six Ph.D.s, and bachelor's programs three Ph.D.s). The Utah State Board of Regents requires data analyses in the form of projections of both "student FTE enrollments and the mean student FTE/faculty FTE ratio for each of the first five years of the program."

Several states handle the explosion of information as both a problem and an opportunity. New Jersey, for instance, is currently considering a revision of its procedures for new programs to include a distinction between routine proposals and proposals with implications for policy. The "fast-track review" has several streamlining mechanisms that result in a review requiring two or three months, while the "comprehensive review," which includes mandatory external consultants, takes six or seven months. Virginia's information and planning environment is such that the agency notes in its initial statement of policy the opportunity inherent in interinstitutional planning:

The Council encourages educational institutions, both public and private, to collaborate in offering degree programs, either cooperatively or jointly. A cooperative *program is one that leads to a degree from an institution [that] draws minimally upon certain resources (such as facilities, curricula, and faculty) of another institution. A* joint *program is one in which two or more institutions share such resources relatively equally.*

Summary

Planning and decision making in the development of new academic programs are two of the most complex areas of university administration. The complexity arises from the fact that the initiation of innovation usually begins with an individual faculty member, while the process of extended approval is a function of administrators. The initiation phase defies order and control. Generation of ideas does not lend itself to management or strategic planning. Yet it has become necessary for planning (and planners) to become involved in the development of new programs as early as possible because of such factors as the proliferation of programs and fiscal constraints. Richard Cyert, president of Carnegie-Mellon, has discussed the general problems involved: "Planning works best when it has been shaped to a great extent by the faculty. However, there will be no planning at all without discipline being imposed upon the organization from a central source. Nobody likes to plan. Faculty members . . . are not great risk takers. Many moved into academic life because they want certainty and security. Thus, the planning process must be initiated from the president's office'' (Keller 1983, p. 90). Planning and decision making for the development of new programs work best therefore with a high level of faculty involvement but under an administratively defined process that involves a clear articulation and communication of mission, the analysis of internal strengths and external opportunities, and the act of establishing specific priorities for the program.

A number of insights result from the review of the literature on planning for and making decisions about new academic programs:

1. The process of identifying internal strengths and translating them into a decision-oriented strategic plan is still very haphazard in colleges and universities. If successful new programs are to be built on internal strengths, less ambiguity about critical self-assessment is needed. Such devices as annual reviews, accreditation exercises, program reviews, program audits, program data, and so on need to be coordinated into an efficient planning process. Without this coordination, every report, review, or audit will be viewed as an independent event. The authors of such self-assessment devices quickly learn to discount their potential value for decision making and merely compile the statistics. A coordinated, integrated approach in which each bit of information builds on another, resulting in specific value judgments, can have major consequences on a program's quality, the allocation of resources, and the development of new programs.

2. External considerations in the development of new programs have received little attention in the literature on higher education, but the situation evidently is changing. Too much attention is being drawn to such issues as economic development, societal responsibilities, and accountability for colleges and universities to remain largely closed systems. The public, students, and legislators are making unprecedented demands on colleges and universities. They want to be assured that academic programs will meet their needs, not just provide a degree. In that regard, four-year colleges and universities should look to some of the practices that our nation's community col-

leges have adopted. Such mechanisms as needs assessment, program support offices, and comprehensive checklists for new programs are potentially valuable because they contain a "boundary-spanning" view of the organization. These practices are proactive, seeking to generate information on the needs and wants of various constituencies.

3. Colleges and universities must begin to see their program offerings as a conscious set of choices that have been determined as the vehicles to carry out their chosen mission. To that end, data must come from both internal and external sources, and they must be in such a form as to allow comparability and analyses of trends. A strategic orientation results from administrators who are able to take such information and match programs with markets. Doing so requires active decision making in which "building, holding, and termination" strategies are the natural outgrowth of the flow of information. Without such setting of priorities and selectivity, gathering information is reduced to a rote exercise, the status quo becomes more entrenched, and the development of new academic programs occurs at the whim and fancy of interested individuals.

4. The nature and scope of the state's and the system's involvement in the development of new programs should be of concern to college and university administrators. The content of an institution's instructional offerings has been at the core of what constitutes a college or university's community of scholars. But as the detail of evaluative criteria expands (applied to majors, minors, concentrations, and so on, involving postprogram approval) at the state and system levels, it is questionable as to who is designing what, which is not to say that state and system agencies should not have an expanded role in approval but that the driving force behind such involvement should be concerned mainly with issues of duplication as they relate to fiscal responsibilities. Colleges and universities must reassure these agencies that they are capable of making informed choices, that they are responsive to social and economic conditions, and that they have the ability to plan and reallocate funds to support those plans.

5. The processes involved in the development of new academic programs must be specific to the institution. Too much variability exists across institutions to believe that

an eight-stage process, or any other lock-step approach, would be of any great use. It has been shown, for example, that proposals for new programs can come from a single faculty member, a small group of professors formed to explore mutual interests, industry leaders, or an innovation fund. But while no universal template exists for developing programs, certain standard rules of thumb, when combined, constitute an orientation toward *planning*. Such notions as information flows, mission statements, "matching," and setting priorities are powerful elements common to all effective processes for the development of new academic programs.

Historically, the development of new programs has been based upon one implicit assumption: growth. The decisions about which new programs to offer were a function of the faculty's interest, the program's relative place in the queue, and the amount of increased funding expected. In today's environment, we face external demands for accountability and internal fiscal constraints. Yet societal conditions and educational disciplines are changing more rapidly than ever. Administrators, professors, trustees, and state education officials must rely on information, innovation, and decision making to ensure that a college or university's academic program portfolio reflects the strengths of the institution and the needs of modern society.

IMPROVING THE PROCESS

The Existing Vacuum

Innovation, strategic planning, evaluation and assessment, and program planning can be visualized as an overlapping set of topics related to the development of new academic programs, and the research and writings included in these areas provide a wealth of useful ideas regarding the innovation of academic programs—ideas that can be translated into more efficient and effective programming in colleges and universities. One obvious conclusion, however, is that a limited amount of descriptive and prescriptive literature specific to the development of new programs is available. The reasons for this vacuum are several. First, "accountability" has never been a popular word in higher education. Not until recently have management systems been put into place that enable legislators, board officials, and administrators to make comparative judgments about the relative quality of academic programs—whether continuing or new. Second, ideas for new programs historically have "bubbled up" from the faculty in a discipline-specific fashion. Therefore, the business programs of the 1960s have become the marketing, product marketing, service marketing, and advertising departments of today. And third, since the end of World War II, higher education has been the quintessential growth industry. In such an environment, more concern understandably is shown about whether the institution has the means to respond to growth than the methods by which it happens. The combination of these three phenomena largely accounts for the fact that we have seen a great deal of activity involving new programs but little understanding of how to do it well.

To sharpen the focus on the means and methods of "improving the process," this final section is concerned with two questions: (1) What factors are associated with success in the development of new academic programs? and (2) What are some specific prescriptions that can be used to ensure the vitality of new program development in colleges and universities? Such a practical perspective should help both administrators and faculty members to create an innovative environment for the development, management, and evaluation of new academic programs.

Factors for Success

The previous section presented the results of a survey of administrators and faculty members involved in the development of new academic programs. While much of that survey was

We have seen a great deal of activity involving new programs but little understanding of how to do it well.

concerned with "planning styles," the final portion of the survey contained some straightforward questions: What is the rating of each factor associated with the success of new programs in terms of *importance* as they apply to your program? What is the one most important factor related to the success of the program and why? The factors were rated with three response categories: most important, neutral, and least important.

Table 10 contains the results of rating 13 factors for success. Of obvious interest is the fact that the two most important factors are concerned with administrative support by a wide margin. The dominant factor is the support of a specific individual who is an enthusiastic believer in the success of the idea, and some respondents were strongly convinced of that importance:

The key to success was the support of a senior official at a key point in the process of getting funding support for equipment and new faculty.

The president of the university!

Support from central administration. Why? This is an essential first step. Nothing else happens if this support is not present.

Interestingly, these first two factors correspond to the primary factors enumerated in a recent report (Duerr 1986). In that corporate survey of "factors associated with success in new product development," the most critical factor was "top management's support for development," and the next factor was "an enthusiastic product manager." It would appear that, regardless of the kind of organization, a champion of the new product is the most essential ingredient.

While a "large and flexible budget" may be an obvious choice, it is intriguing that the same factor ranked last in Duerr's list of 14 factors. It is even more noteworthy, given that the availability of money was barely mentioned when respondents were asked about "the one most important factor." Without getting too speculative, it might be suggested that the environments for innovation in the corporate world and in higher education are reversed. In a large corporation, if you have a good idea, you don't worry about the money. Someone somewhere in the organization will fund it—the idea will find the money. In higher education, however, flexible sources of

TABLE 10

FACTORS ASSOCIATED WITH SUCCESS IN DEVELOPING NEW ACADEMIC PROGRAMS

```
        0    10   20   30   40   50   60   70   80   90  100
        ├─┼─┼─┼─┼─┼─┼─┼─┼─┼─┼─┼─┼─┼─┼─┼─┼─┼─┼─┼─┤
```

Enthusiastic dean
or senior official
————————————————————————————————95%*
--4%

Support of central
administration
————————————————————————78%
---5%

Large and flexible
budget
——————————————50%
---------17%

New program
built on an
existing one
—————————————48%
----------------26%

Successful ex-
perience with
new program
————————————44%
---------17%

Preapproval
criteria
——————————39%
-----------------30%

Clear lines of
authority
—————————35%
------8%

Nonmonetary
incentives
—————————35%
---------17%

Incremental
approach
————————33%
-------------- 22%

Tight control
of expenses
———————30%
------- 10%

Monetary
incentives
——————27%
------------------26%

Decentralized
responsibility
—————25%
-----------------------39%

Alternative
plans
——————17%
-------------------------- 42%

——— Most important
----- Least important

*That is, 95 percent of respondents thought that an enthusiastic dean or senior official was the most important factor in the development of new academic programs; 4 percent thought it was the least important.

funding are much more limited. Fewer guarantees exist that someone will recognize the proposal as worthy of an investment. Consequently, the scenario may be reversed—the money will find ideas.

The strong showing of "new program built on an existing one" suggests that the most successful strategy is an incremental one that progresses from the inside out. One respondent noted the importance of internal strengths and capabilities: "Our university has strong science and engineering talents capable of dealing with new space programs. The National Space Transportation System (shuttle), regular flights to space, a space station program planning for permanent human presence in space provided opportunities for aggressive university involvement. Both faculty and students were ready to go." Again, it is interesting to note that the corporate respondents in Duerr's report rated "new business closely related to old" as the third most important factor. It is apparently important in both environments to know what one does well and then expand on it.

While "preapproval criteria" (expected grants, number of students, and so on) was ranked relatively high in terms of importance, it also received the third largest response for "least important." One respondent noted that the most important factor related to the program's success was the "apparent demand for graduates of the program in the private sector. This [demand] secures enrollment by good students, which in turn secures the faculty interest and administrative support to make the program a success." Such pragmatism may well be in short supply in a college or university, thereby explaining the significant response for "least important."

The two factors that were rated the lowest as "most important" were "decentralized responsibility" and "alternative plans." Decentralization is of concern because all the literature on organizational management suggests that such freedom is crucial to the process of innovation. This result is confirmed in Duerr's report, which shows decentralization of responsibility as one of the most important factors among corporate respondents. This result, while interesting, may simply be a question of academics' taking for granted their high degree of autonomy.

Practical Prescriptions
This final part offers a series of prescriptions to those in a college or university who have an interest in improving the pro-

cess for developing new academic programs. These prescriptions are based upon recurrent themes or specific findings identified in the literature on higher education.

1. *Create and maintain a climate for innovation of programs.* The leadership (including state and system level) of an institution must create a climate that can overcome vested interests, shake up the status quo, fight political territorialism, and generate resources to fuel innovative ideas. The leadership must set priorities, perhaps damaging egos in the process. The criticality of leadership's role is evident in the survey results that showed "enthusiastic dean or senior official" and "central administrative support" as the factors of greatest importance to the success of a new program. The "climate for innovation" begins at the top.

2. *Bring innovative people into the institution.* We tend to forget that all the individuals currently employed at a college or university at one time or another applied for their position. They were interviewed and checked. Unfortunately, higher education search committees often focus on credentials and experience to the exclusion of other qualifications. The characteristics of successful change agents are well documented, and there is no reason why an institution cannot incorporate such characteristics into job descriptions—especially those for administrative positions. It is essential to remember that one of the most important characteristics of innovative organizations is that the individuals within the organization have a positive attitude toward change.

3. *Move innovative people around in the institution.* Complacency and comfortableness work hand in hand. Lifetime appointments, like those resulting from the tenure system, have many advantages but also can create mental stagnation. All of the forces that contribute to stability in personality or in social systems influence the rate of innovation. The use of term appointments for professors, visiting professorships, part-timers, and joint appointments can bring a healthy dose of fresh air to a college or university. Assistant dean, assistant vice president, and assistant to the president are the kinds of positions to which innovative faculty members can be recruited for, say, three years. Again, credentials and experience, while important, should not necessarily be given more weight than a whole range of personal characteristics, including a sense of humor and a willingness to listen to others.

4. *Guard against the trend toward increasing fragmenta-*

tion. As college and university professors continue to specialize in their research, the tendency is to translate those interests into the development of curricula. And in a no-growth environment where new programs are added but far fewer discontinued, allocation of resources can become a problem. In combination, the result can be the loss of critical mass—an institution dominated by far too many small, underfunded programs. Individuals in such departments or programs can easily become isolated and disillusioned. In the same sense, any attempt to foster integrating mechanisms should be encouraged. Such mechanisms entail anything that disrupts a narrow focus on discipline and positively influences the horizontal flow of communications. Some of the most exciting program initiatives occur on the fringes of disciplines, in areas that overlap with other disciplines.

5. *Develop the means to look outward.* Virtually all signs point toward the fact that outside constituencies have increasingly greater expectations for colleges and universities. Yet external influences have often been thought of (in the past) as threats to the independence of higher education. The survey on new programs illustrates, however, that such forces can be important allies to the continuing vitality of institutions. By formalizing and institutionalizing such means as consortia of industries and faculty, lists of experts, and advisory boards, both faculty members and administrators will be in a position to span the boundaries of their colleges and universities. Four-year colleges and universities can take a page from community colleges in this regard.

6. *Separate the idea stage from the approval stage.* The development of a new program usually emerges from the faculty, yet we know that such organizational characteristics as increased formalization and centralization all work to impede the process of innovation. Initiation of innovation must be given full latitude to try an experimental course, work through improbable combinations, conduct surveys, organize intrainstitutional and interinstitutional "exploration" committees. The process of approval functions better in a formal, centralized environment, given the need for decisive decision making. Indeed, faculty members should be insulated from many of the procedural steps inherent in today's extended process of program approval.

7. *Coordinate all activities related to program development through a limited number of persons or offices.* Depending

upon the size of the institution, the responsibility for monitoring a new program, from initiation through institutionalization, should remain with a single individual (e.g., the associate vice president of academic affairs) or a single office (e.g., program development and evaluation). Such an individual or office is a "structural link," accommodating faculty interests with administrative procedures. Given the increased time in the development process (often two to three years) and the vastly increased steps and complexity in state and system reviews, it is especially important that continuity be maintained. By incorporating program reviews in the same office, the institution can begin to bring a strategic orientation to all program evaluation—from development to review to discontinuance.

8. *Integrate institutional research into all procedures for program development.* In reviewing those planning styles that deal with *how* academic planning is done, it is evident that information plays a key role in all of them. While the "program data" style is the most dependent upon institutional information, all of the others benefit from various types of information. As such, the role of institutional research involves not only that of a structural link between the administration and faculty members but also that of a change agent. It is clearly important, therefore, that the person who fills the position for institutional research have characteristics of a change agent and be plugged into all aspects of the development of new programs. Again, given that both internal and external procedures for approval have become so information intensive, the role of institutional research in managing academic information is crucial to effective development of new programs.

9. *Visualize the development of new programs as a continuous, dynamic process.* Academic program planning was presented as a three-stage cycle in which programs were conceived, flourished, and were discontinued. While it may be impossible for some to think of English, history, or physics as being discontinued, no program should be seen as having an inalienable right to exist. As the mission of a college or university changes, it is fundamental that programs are added and subtracted to reflect the future direction of the institution. The adoption of such planning tools as product life cycles and product portfolios stresses the dynamism of program evolution. Without such an orientation, the glorification of the status quo becomes the dominant cultural theme.

10. *Develop a selective strategy.* If the proper climate exists

in the institution, numbers of ideas for new programs should continually be proposed. And a few existing programs will have lost their purpose, dropped in demand, become too expensive, or declined below a minimal level of quality. Consequently, colleges and universities must have methods to compare proposed programs with existing programs. Comparative judgments concerning the optimal allocation of resources should result in a selective strategy in which priorities are the obvious outcome. Institutions can no longer afford to let academic programs evolve haphazardly. The process must be planned—strategically.

11. *Integrate planning for academic programs with planning for finances and facilities.* The importance of strategic planning that includes both finances and facilities cannot be overemphasized. First, if colleges and universities do not plan strategically, someone else will. But just as important, a new program should not be victimized by a lack of funds before it has had a chance to prove itself. It should not be forced to make do with substandard equipment or limited space. Such constraints will necessarily result in a loss of morale among both faculty and students, create a downturn in quality, and dampen further efforts at innovation.

12. *Coordinate internal and external processes for approval.* With the increased scope of approval for new programs at the state and system levels, the process can develop into the academic equivalent of a 26-mile marathon. The process can be especially lengthy and frustrating if different questions are asked in different ways for different purposes at different levels. Because state and system concerns are somewhat dissimilar to institutional concerns, such a possibility distinctly exists. One way to overcome it is to begin the process with generation of broad-based data. Appendix A illustrates the kind of information that is required in the first section (What would be the general content of the program?) of the seven-section procedural checklist. Such a checklist can be tailored to the institution with state and system evaluative criteria in mind. This approach is particularly useful because it offers program planners a systematic way to think about program proposals as they affect all other areas of the institution. That is, while evaluative criteria are necessary to make choices regarding *whether* a program is viable, such criteria are not necessarily related to understanding *how* a new program will become viable.

Higher education finds itself in an environment where the development of new academic programs can have a demonstrably negative or positive effect. Program development that is not actively and creatively supported will be overwhelmed by the forces of the status quo. And perhaps as much a concern, development that is allowed to proceed unmanaged will usually gravitate toward the narrow, isolated interests of a few individuals. Such programs can extend the resources of the institution, making it difficult for administrators to find the flexibility to follow any type of selective strategy. In contrast, new programs that coincide with the institution's mission, that leverage internal strengths, that support the quality of life in the state and the region, and that are properly planned and funded are a prime source of continuing institutional vitality.

APPENDIX A

AN (ABRIDGED) PROCEDURAL CHECKLIST:
What Would Be the General Content of the program?

Philosophy and Goals
- PURPOSES: What are the major purposes of the program?
  - Personal/social needs of students: What personal/social needs of the students should the program meet?
  - Community needs: What manpower or human service needs of the community should the program meet?
  - Career development needs of students: What career development needs of students should the program meet?
- OCCUPATIONAL GOALS: For what occupational tasks should training be provided?
- GENERAL EDUCATIONAL GOALS: What general educational goals should the program meet? What personal, social, or occupational goals of the student should general education meet?
- PROFESSIONAL GOALS: What are the professional goals of the program?
  - Accreditation and licensure: Should the program meet accreditation or licensure criteria of any institution or organization?
  - Certification: Should the graduates of the program be prepared to pass certification tests?
  - Entry tests: Should the graduates of the program be prepared to pass entry tests for any occupation?
  - Advanced degrees: Should the graduates of the program be prepared to enter other institutions that offer more advanced degrees?

Curriculum
- EXPECTATIONS FOR ENTERING STUDENTS:
  - Knowledge: What areas of knowledge are entering students anticipated to know?
  - Competencies: What competencies are entering students expected to have?
  - Attitudes and values: What attitudes and values are entering students expected to have?
- INTENDED LEARNING OUTCOMES: What are the intended learning outcomes of the program?
  - Knowledge: What are the major areas of knowledge that need to be taught in the program?
  - Competencies: What are the major types of competencies that need to be acquired in the program?
  - Attitudes and values: What attitudes and values need to be fostered in the program?
- COURSES: What courses will make up the program?

- Requirements: What specific courses will be required?
- Electives: What electives might complement the occupational goals of the program? What electives might meet the personal or social needs of the students?
- Remedial work: If students entering the program do not have the expected knowledge, skills, or attitudes, will remedial work, tutoring, and/or academic counseling be available?

Instructional Plan
- GENERAL TEACHING STRATEGIES:
  - For knowledge: What teaching strategies will be used to cover the major areas of knowledge?
  - For competencies: What teaching strategies will be used to develop competencies in occupational tasks? (Such strategies might include field experience, laboratory work, or cooperative education.)
  - For attitudes and values: What teaching strategies will be used to instill or develop the desirable attitudes and values?
- SPECIAL TEACHING STRATEGIES: Will any special teaching strategies be used in the program?
  - Internships and labwork: Does the program include internships, extensive laboratory work, or field experience?
  - Cooperative education: Does the program include cooperative education or work study experience?
  - Modular curriculum: Will the curriculum be written in modular form? Will the teaching strategy include modular scheduling?

Source: Beilby and Corwin 1976. (Refer to Beilby and Corwin for the full seven-section checklist and supporting materials.)

REFERENCES

The Educational Resources Information Center (ERIC) Clearinghouse
on Higher Education abstracts and indexes the current literature on
higher education for inclusion in ERIC's data base and announcement
in ERIC's monthly bibliographic journal, *Resources in Education*
(RIE). Most of these publications are available through the ERIC
Document Reproduction Service (EDRS). For publications cited in this
bibliography that are available from EDRS, ordering number and price
are included. Readers who wish to order a publication should write to
the ERIC Document Reproduction Service, 3900 Wheeler Avenue,
Alexandria, Virginia 22304. (Phone orders with VISA or MasterCard
are taken at 800/227-ERIC or 703/823-0500.) When ordering, please
specify the document (ED) number. Documents are available as noted
in microfiche (MF) and paper copy (PC). Because prices are subject to
change, it is advisable to check the lastest issue of *Resources in
Education* for current cost based on the number of pages in the
publication.

Abell, D.F., and J.S. Hammond. 1979. *Strategic Market Planning*.
Englewood Cliffs, N.J.: Prentice Hall.

Abrams, Robert, et al. 1983. *Preparing for High Technology: CAD/
CAM Programs*. Columbus, Ohio: National Center for Research in
Vocational Education. ED 228 473. 85 pp. MF–$1.07; PC–$10.13.

Academy for Educational Development. 1984. *Revitalization and
Renewal*. New York: Author.

Andrews, Frank M. 1975. "Social and Psychological Factors which
Influence the Creative Process." In *Perspective in Creativity*, edited by
Irving A. Taylor and J.W. Getzels. Chicago: Aldine Publishing Co.

Arns, Robert G., and William Poland. 1980. "Changing the University
through Program Review." *Journal of Higher Education* 51 (3):
268–84.

Balderston, Frederick E. 1981. "Dynamics of Planning: Strategic
Approaches and Higher Education." In *Management Science
Applications to Academic Administration*, edited by J. Wilson. New
Directions for Higher Education No. 35. San Francisco: Jossey-
Bass.

Baldridge, J. Victor. 1971. *Power and Conflict in the University*. New
York: John Wiley & Sons.

———. 1980. "Managerial Innovation." *Journal of Higher Education* 51 (2): 117–34.

Baldridge, J. Victor, and Robert A. Burnham. June 1975. "Organizational Innovation: Individual, Organizational, and Environmental
Impacts." *Administrative Science Quarterly* 20: 165–76.

Barak, Robert J. 1982. *Program Review in Higher Education*.
Boulder, Colo.: National Center for Higher Education Management
Systems. ED 246 829. 137 pp. MF–$1.07; PC–$14.01.

———. 1986. "A Perspective on the Antecedents, Present Status, and Future Developments of Academic Program Review in Higher Education." Paper presented at an annual meeting of the Association for the Study of Higher Education, San Antonio, Texas. ED 268 887. 34 pp. MF–$1.07; PC–$5.79.

Barak, Robert J., and Robert O. Berdahl. 1977. *State-Level Academic Program Review in Higher Education.* Denver, Colo.: Education Commission of the States.

Beilby, Albert E., and Luene Corwin. 1976. *Curricular Decision Making in Occupational Education: A Procedural Checklist and Guide.* Albany: New York State Education Department. ED 130 728. 115 pp. MF–$1.07; PC–$6.01.

Benne, Kenneth D., Robert Chin, and Warren G. Bennis. 1985. "Planned Change in America." In *The Planning of Change,* 4th rev. ed., edited by Warren G. Bennis, Kenneth D. Benne, and Robert Chin. New York: Holt, Rinehart & Winston.

Bennett, John B. 1983. "What Lies in the Future for Department Chairpersons?" *Educational Record* 64 (2): 52–56.

Benoist, Howard. 1986. "Planning and Academic Program Review." *Planning for Higher Education* 14 (2): 22–25.

Benveniste, Guy. 1985. "New Politics of Higher Education: Hidden and Complex." *Higher Education* 14 (2): 175–95.

Berdahl, Robert O. 1971. *Statewide Coordination of Higher Education.* Washington, D.C.: American Council on Higher Education.

Blau, Judith R., and William McKinley. June 1979. "Ideas, Complexity, and Innovation." *Administrative Science Quarterly* 24: 200–219.

Bloom, Allan. 1987. *The Closing of the American Mind.* New York: Simon & Schuster.

Booz, Allen & Hamilton. 1982. *New Products Management for the 1980s.* New York: Author.

Bowen, Howard R. 1984. "What's Ahead for Higher Education?" *Change* 16 (3): 9–13.

Breier, Barbara E. 1986. "Changes in Program Review: A Case Study." Paper presented at an annual meeting of the Association for the Study of Higher Education, San Antonio, Texas. ED 268 897. 28 pp. MF–$1.07; PC–$5.79.

Brown, David G. Fall 1970. "Criteria for Pruning Programs." *Educational Record:* 405–9.

Brown, Peggy Ann. 1984. *The New Scholarship on Women.* Washington, D.C.: Association of American Colleges. ED 243 374. 21 pp. MF–$1.07; PC not available EDRS.

Burns, Tom, and G.M. Stalker. 1961. *The Management of Innovation.* London: Tavistock Publications.

Cameron, Kim S., Myung U. Kim, and David A. Whetten. 1987.

"Organizational Effects of Decline and Turbulence." *Administrative Science Quarterly* 32 (2): 222–40.

Carnegie Council on Policy Studies in Higher Education. 1980. *Three Thousand Futures: The Next Twenty Years for Higher Education.* San Francisco: Jossey-Bass.

Chaffee, Ellen Earle. 1983. *Rational Decision Making in Higher Education.* Boulder, Colo.: National Center for Higher Education Management Systems. ED 246 828. 92 pp. MF–$1.07; PC–$10.03.

Cherin, Ellen, and Frank Armijo. 1980. *Supplement to the Handbook for Institutional Academic and Program Planning.* Boulder, Colo.: National Center for Higher Education Management Systems. ED 195 220. 443 pp. MF–$1.07; PC not available EDRS.

Chin, Robert, and Kenneth D. Benne. 1985. "General Strategies for Effecting Changes in Human Systems." In *The Planning of Change,* 4th rev. ed., edited by Warren G. Bennis, Kenneth D. Benne, and Robert Chin. New York: Holt, Rinehart & Winston.

Christenson, Donald D. 1982. "Changes in Higher Education: Forces and Impacts." In *Effective Planned Change Strategies,* edited by G. Hipps. New Directions for Institutional Research No. 33. San Francisco: Jossey-Bass.

Clark, Burton R. 1983. "The Contradictions of Change in Academic Systems." *Higher Education* 12 (1): 101–16.

Clark, Mary Jo. 1983. "Academic Program Evaluation." In *Using Research for Strategic Planning*, edited by Norman P. Uhl. New Directions for Institutional Research No. 37. San Francisco: Jossey-Bass.

Clugston, Richard M. 1986. "Strategic Planning in an Organized Anarchy: The Emperor's New Clothes?" Paper presented at an annual meeting of the Association for the Study of Higher Education, San Antonio, Texas. ED 268 902. 35 pp. MF–$1.07, PC–$5.79.

Cohen, Michael D., and James G. March. 1974. *Leadership and Ambiguity.* 2d rev. ed. Boston: Harvard Business School Press.

Conrad, Clifton F., and Richard F. Wilson. 1985. *Academic Program Reviews: Institutional Approaches, Expectations, and Controversies.* ASHE-ERIC Higher Education Report No. 5. Washington, D.C.: Association for the Study of Higher Education. ED 264 806. 111 pp. MF–$1.07; PC–$12.07.

Cope, Robert G. 1981. *Strategic Planning, Management, and Decision Making.* AAHE-ERIC Higher Education Research Report No. 9. Washington, D.C.: American Association for Higher Education. ED 217 825. 75 pp. MF–$1.07; PC–$7.73.

Craven, Eugene. 1980. "Evaluating Program Performance." In *Improving Academic Management,* edited by Paul Jedamus, Marvin Peterson, and Associates. San Francisco: Jossey-Bass.

Crawford, C.M. 1979. "Marketing Research and the New Product Failure Rate." *Journal of Marketing* 41 (2): 67–79.

Cyert, Richard M. 1978. "The Management of Universities of Constant or Decreasing Size." *Public Administration Review* 38 (4): 344–49.

———. 1981. "Management Science and University Management." In *Management Science Applications to Academic Administration*, edited by J. Wilson. New Directions for Higher Education No. 35. San Francisco: Jossey-Bass.

Daft, Richard, and Selwyn Becker. 1978. *Innovation in Organizations*. New York: Elsevier.

Davis, Robert H., et al. 1982. "The Impact of Organizational and Innovator Variables on Instructional Innovation in Higher Education." *Journal of Higher Education* 53 (5): 568–86.

Denney, Clifford O., Nancy L. Conrath, and D. Robert Stiff. 1979. "Comprehensive Program Assessment by Students in a Multicampus District." *Planning for Higher Education* 7 (4): 1–6.

Dressel, Paul. 1976. *Handbook of Academic Evaluation: Assessing Institutional Effectiveness, Student Progress, and Professional Performance for Decision Making in Higher Education*. San Francisco: Jossey-Bass.

———. 1987. "Mission, Organization, and Leadership." *Journal of Higher Education* 58 (1): 101–9.

Drucker, Peter F. 1985. *Innovation and Entrepreneurship*. New York: Harper & Row.

Duerr, Michael G. 1986. *The Commercial Development of New Products*. New York: Conference Board.

Duncan, Robert. 1972. "Organizational Climate and Climate for Change in Three Police Departments: Some Preliminary Findings." *Urban Affairs Quarterly* 8 (2): 205–45.

El-Khawas, Elaine. 1985. "Campuses Weld the Corporate Link." *Educational Record* 66 (2): 37–39.

Ellstrom, P.E. 1983. "Four Faces of Educational Organizations." *Higher Education* 12 (2): 231–41.

Evans, Richard I. 1982. "Resistance to Innovations in Information Technology in Higher Education: A Social Psychological Perspective." In *Information Technology: Innovations and Applications* New Directions for Institutional Research No. 35. San Francisco: Jossey-Bass.

Evans, Richard I., and P. Leppman. 1968. *Resistance to Innovation in Higher Education*. San Francisco: Jossey-Bass.

Fessler, D.R. 1976. *Facilitating Community Change: A Basic Guide*. La Jolla, Cal.: Univ. Associates.

Floyd, Carol Everly. 1985. *Faculty Participation in Decision Making: Necessity or Luxury?* ASHE-ERIC Higher Education Report No. 8.

Washington, D.C.: Association for the Study of Higher Education. ED 267 694. 119 pp. MF–$1.07; PC–$12.07.

Folger, John K. 1977. *Increasing the Public Accountability of Higher Education.* New Directions for Institutional Research No. 16. San Francisco: Jossey-Bass.

Foster, M.J. 1983. "Portfolio Analysis in the Planning of Higher Education." *Higher Education* 12 (4): 389–97.

Franklin, Phyllis. 1982. "Institutional Strategies: Duke University." *Educational Record* 63 (3): 34–38.

Freeman, Thomas M., and William A. Simpson. 1980. "Using Institutional Data to Plan Academic Programs: A Case History." In *Academic Planning for the 1980s,* edited by Richard B. Heydinger. New Directions for Institutional Research No. 28. San Francisco: Jossey-Bass.

Gaff, Jerry G. Fall 1980. "Avoiding the Potholes: Strategies for Reforming General Education." *Educational Record*: 50–59.

Gardner, John W. 1964. *Self-Renewal: The Individual and the Innovative Society.* New York: Harper & Row.

Gillis, Arthur L. 1982. "Planning Choice/Resource Compaction." *Planning for Higher Education* 10 (3): 33–38.

Glover, Robert H., and Jeffrey Holmes. 1983. "Assessing the External Environment." In *Using Research for Strategic Planning,* edited by N.P. Uhl. New Directions for Institutional Research No. 37. San Francisco: Jossey-Bass.

Groves, Roderick T. 1979. "Program Review in a Multilevel State Governance System: The Case of Illinois." *Planning for Higher Education* 8 (1): 1–9.

Gushkin, Alan E., and Michael A. Bassis. 1985. "Leadership Styles and Institutional Renewal." In *Leadership and Institutional Renewal,* edited by R.M. Davis. New Directions for Higher Education No. 49. San Francisco: Jossey-Bass.

Hackman, Judith Dozier. 1985. "Power and Centrality in the Allocation of Resources in Colleges and Universities." *Administrative Science Quarterly* 30 (1): 61–77.

Hage, Jerald, and Michael Aiken. 1967. "Program Change and Organizational Properties: A Comparative Analysis." *American Journal of Sociology* 72 (5): 503–19.

———. 1970. *Social Change in Complex Organizations.* New York: Random House.

Harvey, Edward, and Russell Mills. 1970. "Patterns of Organizational Adaptation: A Political Perspective." In *Power in Organizations,* edited by Mayer N. Zald. Nashville: Vanderbilt Univ. Press.

Havelock, Ronald G. 1973. *The Change Agent's Guide to Innovation in Education.* Englewood Cliffs, N.J.: Educational Technology Productions.

Havelock, Ronald G., and Mary C. Havelock. 1973. *Training for Change Agents.* Ann Arbor: Univ. of Michigan, Institute for Social Research.

Hefferlin, J.B. 1969. *Dynamics of Academic Reform.* San Francisco: Jossey-Bass.

Henderson, Algo D. 1970. *The Innovative Spirit.* San Francisco: Jossey-Bass.

Hesburgh, Theodore M. 1971. "The Nature of the Challenge: Traditional Organization and Attitude of Universities toward Contemporary Realities." In *The Task of Universities in a Changing World*, edited by Stephen D. Kertesz. Notre Dame, Ind.: Univ. of Notre Dame Press.

Hewton, Eric. 1982. *Rethinking Educational Change.* Guilford, Eng.: Society for Research into Higher Education.

Heydinger, Richard B. 1980a. "Introduction: Academic Program Planning in Perspective." In *Academic Planning for the 1980s*, edited by Richard B. Heydinger. New Directions for Institutional Research No. 28. San Francisco: Jossey-Bass.

———. 1980b. "Planning Academic Programs." In *Improving Academic Management,* edited by Paul Jedamus, Marvin W. Peterson, and Associates. San Francisco: Jossey-Bass.

Hodgkinson, Harold L. 1971. *Institutions in Transition.* New York: McGraw-Hill.

Hollowood, James R. 1981. "College and University Strategic Planning: A Methodological Approach." *Planning for Higher Education* 9 (4): 8–18.

Holt, Hamilton. Nov. 1930. "We Venture on New Paths." *Journal of Higher Education* 11: 503–7.

Howard, John, and Jagdish Sheth. 1969. *The Theory of Buyer Behavior.* New York: John Wiley & Sons.

Humphries, Jack W. 1983. "Academic Program Review." Paper presented at the Annual Meeting of the Rocky Mountain Association for Institutional Research, Taos, New Mexico. ED 238 351. 18 pp. MF–$1.07; PC–$3.85.

Jellema, William W. 1986. "The Legacy of Rip van Winkle." In *Institutional Revival: Case Histories*, edited by D.W. Steeples. New Directions for Higher Education No. 54. San Francisco: Jossey-Bass.

Kahn, Robert, Donald Wolfe, J.D. Snoek, and Richard Rosenthal. 1964. *Organizational Stress: Studies in Role Conflict and Ambiguity.* New York: John Wiley & Sons.

Karber, David J., and Donald A. MacPhee. 1980. "Planning for 1979 and Beyond: A Process for Studying Program Viability." *Planning for Higher Education* 8 (3): 27–30.

Katz, Daniel, and Robert L. Kahn. 1978. *The Social Psychology of Organizations.* 2d rev. ed. New York: John Wiley & Sons.

Keller, George. 1983. *Academic Strategy.* Baltimore: Johns Hopkins Univ. Press.

Kieft, Raymond N., Frank Armijo, and Neil S. Bucklew. 1978. *A Handbook for Institutional Academic and Program Planning: From Idea to Implementation.* Boulder, Colo.: National Center for Higher Education Management Systems. ED 161 327. 80 pp. MF–$1.07; PC–$10.03.

Kotler, Philip. 1982. *Marketing for Nonprofit Organizations.* 2d rev. ed. Englewood Cliffs, N.J.: Prentice Hall.

Kotler, Philip, and Patrick E. Murphy. 1981. "Strategic Planning for Higher Education." *Journal of Higher Education* 52 (5): 470–89.

Leavitt, Harold J. 1965. "Applied Organizational Change in Industry: Structural, Technological, and Humanistic Approaches." In *Handbook of Organizations,* edited by James G. March. Chicago: Rand McNally.

Lee, Wayne A., and Joseph E. Gilmour, Jr. 1977. "A Procedure for the Development of New Programs in Postsecondary Education." *Journal of Higher Education* 48 (3): 304–20.

Lenning, O.T., et al. 1977. *A Structure for the Outcomes of Post-secondary Education.* Boulder, Colo.: National Center for Higher Education Management Systems. ED 150 904. 86 pp. MF–$1.07; PC–$10.03.

Levine, Arthur. 1978. *Handbook on Undergraduate Curriculum.* San Francisco: Jossey-Bass.

———. 1980. *Why Innovation Fails.* Albany: State Univ. of New York Press.

Lincoln, Yvonna S. 1986. "Indigenous Efforts at Individualizing Program Review: A Case Study." Paper presented at an annual meeting of the Association for the Study of Higher Education, San Antonio, Texas. ED 268 892. 21 pp. MF–$1.07; PC–$3.85.

Lincoln, Yvonna S., and Jane Tuttle. 1983. "Centrality as a Prior Criterion." Paper presented at a joint meeting of the Association for the Study of Higher Education and the American Educational Research Association, San Francisco, California. ED 240 934. 15 pp. MF–$1.07; PC–$3.85.

Lindquist, J. May 1974. "Political Linkage: The Academic-Innovation Process." *Journal of Higher Education* 45: 323–43.

———. 1978. *Strategies for Change.* Berkeley, Cal.: Pacific Soundings Press.

Lippitt, Ronald, et al. 1973. "Design for a Research Utilization System for the Social and Rehabilitation Service." In *A Report to the Social and Rehabilitation Service,* edited by Ronald Havelock. Ann Arbor: Univ. of Michigan, Center for Research on Utilization of Scientific Knowledge.

Lippitt, Ronald, Jean Watson, and Bruce Wesley. 1958. *The Dynamics of Planned Change.* New York: Harcourt, Brace, Jovanovich.

Little, Blair. 1984. "Significant Issues for the Future of Product Innovation." *Journal of Product Innovation Management* 1 (1): 56–66.

Long, James P. May 1983. "Industry Speaks to Two-Year Colleges about High Technology." *Viewpoints* 20. ED 231 492. 8 pp. MF–$1.07; PC–$3.85.

Lundy, Harold W. 1985. "A Closer Look at Cost Behavior Patterns and the Implementation of New Programs." Paper presented at the Annual Forum of the Association for Institutional Research, Portland, Oregon. ED 259 672. 46 pp. MF–$1.07; PC–$5.79.

Lynton, Ernest A. 1982. "Corporate Education: College Opportunity." *AGB Reports* 24 (1): 42–46.

———. 1983. "Reexamining the Role of the University." *Change* 15 (7): 19–23 +.

McFadden, G. Bruce, and Susan D. Cohen. 1984. "Community Hospitals and Universities: An Uneasy Partnership." *Educational Record* 65 (4): 53–55.

McMillan, Liz. 1988. "On Many Campuses, 'Strategic Planning' Leads to Streamlined Programs and New Images." *Chronicle of Higher Education* 34 (20): A15–A17.

Magrath, C. Peter. 1980. "The State Connection." *Educational Record* 61 (4): 68–71.

———. 1986. "The Great Teacher Education Talkathon." *Educational Record* 67 (4): 7–11.

Manns, Curtis, and James G. March. 1978. "Financial Adversity, Internal Competition, and Curriculum Change in a University." *Administrative Science Quarterly* 23 (4): 541–52.

March, James, and Herbert Simon. 1958. *Organizations.* New York: John Wiley & Sons.

Martens, Freda R. 1985. "Students, Faculty, and Programs in State University of New York Community Colleges." Albany: State Univ. of New York. ED 264 903. 22 pp. MF–$1.07; PC–$3.85.

Martin, Warren Bryan. 1969. *Conformity: Standards and Change in Higher Education.* San Francisco: Jossey-Bass.

Martorana, S.V., and Eileen Kuhns. 1975. *Managing Academic Change: Interactive Forces and Leadership in Higher Education.* San Francisco: Jossey-Bass.

Mason, Thomas R. 1984. "The Search for Quality in the Face of Retrenchment: Planning for Program Consolidation within Resource Capacities." Paper presented at the Annual International Conference of the Society for College and University Planning, Cambridge, Massachusetts. ED 248 756. 27 pp. MF–$1.07; PC–$5.79.

Maxwell, G.W., and Linda Nunes West. 1980. *Handbook for Developing Competency-Based Curricula for New and Emerging Occupations.* Sacramento: California State Department of Education. ED 210 518. 104 pp. MF–$1.07; PC–$12.07.

Mayhew, Lewis B. 1979. *Surviving the Eighties*. San Francisco: Jossey-Bass.

Melchiori, Gerlinda S. 1982. *Planning for Program Discontinuance: From Default to Design*. AAHE-ERIC Higher Education Research Report No. 5. Washington, D.C.: American Association for Higher Education. ED 224 451. 58 pp. MF–$1.07; PC–$7.73.

Millard, Richard M. 1980. "Power of State Coordinating Agencies." In *Improving Academic Management*, edited by Paul Jedamus, Marvin W. Peterson, and Associates. San Francisco: Jossey-Bass.

Miller, Howard J. 1986. "Interinstitutional Cooperation: A Planning Strategy for Achieving Academic Program Development." *Viewpoints*. ED 271 041. 22 pp. MF–$1.07; PC–$3.85.

Miller, Richard I., and Robert J. Barak. 1986. "Rating Undergraduate Program Review at the State Level." *Educational Record* 67 (2–3): 42–46.

Millett, John. 1984. *Conflict in Higher Education: State Government Coordination versus Institutional Independence*. San Francisco: Jossey-Bass.

Mims, R. Sue. 1980. "Resource Allocation: Stopgap or Support for Academic Planning." In *Academic Planning for the 1980s*, edited by Richard B. Heydinger. New Directions for Institutional Research No. 28. San Francisco: Jossey-Bass.

Mingle, James R. 1982. *Redirecting Higher Education in a Time of Budget Reduction: Issues in Higher Education*. Atlanta: Southern Regional Education Board. ED 214 486. 9 pp. MF–$1.07; PC–$3.85.

Missouri State Coordinating Board for Higher Education. 1983. *Trends in Instructional Programs at Missouri Public Four-Year Institutions, 1972–1982*. Jefferson City: Author. ED 248 809. 73 pp. MF–$1.07; PC–$7.73.

Mohr, Lawrence B. 1969. "Determinants of Innovation in Organizations." *American Political Science Review* 63 (1): 111–26.

Mooney, Carolyn J. 1987. "No Joke: Higher Education in New Jersey Thrives along with State Economy." *Chronicle of Higher Education* 34 (7): A20–A21.

Morrison, James L. 1985. "Establishing an Environmental Scanning Process." In *Leadership and Institutional Renewal*. New Directions for Higher Education No. 49. San Francisco: Jossey-Bass.

Newman, Frank. 1987. *Choosing Quality: Reducing Conflict between the State and the University*. Denver: Education Commission of the States.

Nordvall, Robert C. 1982. *The Process of Change in Higher Education Institutions*. AAHE-ERIC Higher Education Research Report No. 7. Washington, D.C.: American Association for Higher Education. ED 225 472. 58 pp. MF–$1.07; PC–$7.73.

Normann, Richard. 1971. "Organizational Innovativeness: Product

Variation and Reorientation." *Administrative Science Quarterly* 16 (2): 203–15.

Ohio Board of Regents. 1973. *Management Improvement Program.* Columbus: Author. ED 096 877. 96 pp. MF–$1.07; PC–$10.03.

Oliva, L. Jay. 1986. "Faculty Rise to the Challenge Grant." *Educational Record* 67 (4): 44–46.

Peck, Robert D. 1983. "The Entrepreneurial President." *Educational Record* 64 (1): 18–29.

———. 1984. "Entrepreneurship as a Significant Factor in Successful Adaptation." *Journal of Higher Education* 54 (2): 269–85.

———. 1985. "Entrepreneurship and Small-College Leadership." In *Leadership and Institutional Renewal,* edited by R.M. Davis. New Directions for Higher Education No. 49. San Francisco: Jossey-Bass.

Pelczar, Michael J., and Lewis C. Solman. 1984. *Keeping Graduate Programs Responsive to National Needs.* New Directions for Higher Education No. 46. San Francisco: Jossey-Bass.

Peterson, Marvin W. 1980. "Analyzing Alternative Approaches to Planning." In *Improving Academic Management*, edited by Paul Jedamus, Marvin W. Peterson, and Associates. San Francisco: Jossey-Bass.

Rawlings, Hunter R. 1987. "The Basic Mission of Higher Education Is Thwarted by Academic Departments." *Chronicle of Higher Education* 34 (7): B2.

Rehnke, Mary Ann F. 1987. *Creating Career Programs in a Liberal Arts Context.* New Directions for Higher Education No. 57. San Francisco: Jossey-Bass.

Renfro, William L., and James L. Morrison. 1983. "The Scanning Process: Methods and Uses." In *Applying Methods and Techniques of Futures Research.* New Directions for Institutional Research No. 39. San Francisco: Jossey-Bass.

Robertson, Thomas S. 1971. *Innovative Behavior and Communication.* New York: Holt, Rinehart & Winston.

Rogers, Everett M. 1962. *Diffusion of Innovations.* New York: Macmillan.

Rogers, Everett M., and F. Floyd Shoemaker. 1971. *Communication of Innovations: A Cross-Cultural Approach.* New York: Free Press.

Ross, Donald S. 1958. *Administration for Adaptability: A Source Book Drawing Together the Results of More Than 150 Individual Studies Related to the Question of Why and How Schools Improve.* New York: Metropolitan School Study Council.

Rutherford, Desmond, William Fleming, and Haydn Mathias. Aug. 1985. "Strategies for Change in Higher Education: Three Political Models." *Higher Education* 14: 433–45.

Salancik, Gerald R., and Jeffrey Pfeffer. 1974. "The Bases and Use of Power in Organizational Decision Making: The Case of a University." *Administrative Science Quarterly* 19 (4): 453–58.

Salloway, Shirley E., and Martha W. Tack. 1978. "Comprehensive Planning: An Organizational Approach." *Planning for Higher Education* 7 (2): 1–7.

Seymour, Daniel T. 1987. "Out on a Limb: Why Administrators Must Take Risks." *Educational Record* 68 (2): 36–40.

Shepard, Herbert A. 1967. "Innovation-Resisting and Innovation-Producing Organizations." *Journal of Business* 40 (4): 470–77.

Shirley, Robert C., and J. Fredericks Volkwein. 1978. "Establishing Academic Program Priorities." *Journal of Higher Education* 49 (2): 472–88.

Sikes, Walter W., Lawrence E. Schlesinger, and Charles N. Seashore. 1974. *Renewing Higher Education from Within.* San Francisco: Jossey-Bass.

Simpson, William A. 1985. "Easing the Pain of Program Review: Departments Take the Initiative." *Educational Record* 66 (2): 40–42.

Smith, Donald K. 1980. "Preparing for a Decade of Enrollment Decline: The Experience of the University of Wisconsin System." Paper presented at the Legislative Work Conference of the Southern Regional Education Board, Atlanta, Georgia. ED 195 222. 9 pp. MF–$1.07; PC–$3.85.

Smith, Tim R., Mark Drabenstott, and Lynn Gibson. Nov. 1987. "The Role of Universities in Economic Development." *Economic Review:* 3–21.

Steffire, Volney. 1985. "Organizational Obstacles to Innovation: A Formulation of the Problem." *Journal of Product Innovation Management* 2 (2): 3–11.

Stufflebeam, D.L., and W.J. Webster. 1980. "An Analysis of Alternative Approaches to Evaluation." *Educational Evaluation and Policy Analysis* 2 (3): 5–20.

Tack, Martha, Audrey Rentz, and Ronald L. Russell. 1984. "Strategic Planning for Academic Programs: A Strategy for Institutional Survival." *Planning for Higher Education* 12 (4): 8–14.

Terrass, Stuart, and Velma Pomrenke. 1981. "The Institutional Researcher as Change Agent." In *Increasing the Use of Institutional Research*, edited by Jack Lindquist. New Directions for Institutional Research No. 32. San Francisco: Jossey-Bass.

Thompson, Hugh L. 1986. "Evaluating Academic Programs." ED 273 193. 6 pp. MF–$1.07; PC–$3.85.

Thompson, Victor A. 1969. *Bureaucracy and Innovation.* Birmingham: Univ. of Alabama Press.

Torrance, E.P. 1965. "Scientific Views of Creativity and Factors Affecting Its Growth." *Daedalus* 94: 663–82.

Tucker, Allan, and Robert B. Mautz. 1980. "Belling the Academic Cat." *Educational Record* 61 (4): 38–42.

Uhl, Norman P., ed. 1983. *Using Research for Strategic Planning.* New Directions for Institutional Research No. 37. San Francisco: Jossey-Bass.

Van Doren, Doris C., Louise W. Smith, and Ronald J. Biglin. 1986. "Promoting Corporate Enterprise: Marketing the Executive MBA." *Educational Record* 67 (1): 34–39.

Watson, Goodwin. 1972. "Meeting Resistance." In *Creating Social Change,* edited by Gerald Zaltman, Philip Kotler, and Ira Kaufman. New York: Holt, Rinehart & Winston.

Weick, Karl E. 1976. "Educational Organizations as Loosely Coupled Systems." *Administrative Science Quarterly* 21 (1): 1–19.

Whetten, David A. 1980. "Organizational Decline: A Neglected Topic in Organizational Science." *Academy of Management Review* 8 (5): 577–88.

———. 1984. "Effective Administrators: Good Management on the College Campus." *Change* 16 (8): 39–43.

Whyte, William H. 1956. *The Organization Man.* New York: Simon & Schuster.

Wilson, James Q. 1966. "Innovation in Organization: Notes toward a Theory." In *Approaches to Organizational Design*, edited by James D. Thompson. Pittsburgh: Univ. of Pittsburgh Press.

Wilson, Richard F. 1982. *Designing Academic Program Reviews.* New Directions for Higher Education No. 37. San Francisco: Jossey-Bass.

Winstead, Philip C. 1982. "Planned Change in Institutions of Higher Learning." In *Effective Planned Change Strategies*, edited by G. Hipps. New Directions for Institutional Research No. 33. San Francisco: Jossey-Bass.

Zaltman, Gerald, and Robert Duncan. 1977. *Strategies for Planned Change.* New York: John Wiley & Sons.

Zaltman, Gerald, Robert Duncan, and Jonny Holbek. 1973. *Innovations and Organizations.* New York: John Wiley & Sons.

Zaltman, Gerald, et al. 1977. *Dynamic Educational Change.* New York: Free Press.

INDEX

decline, 32
projection, 61, 84, 92
Entrepreneurship
planning style, 53, 56
presidents, 16
Environmental analysis, 64
Environmental scanning, 66
Evaluation
criteria, 43, 63, 64, 81–83
types, 29
Excellence Fund (Oklahoma State U.), 63
Executive MBA, 69, 70
Exit interviews, 60
External influences
corporate, 69–70
foundations, 67, 68
government, 67–68
opportunities, 5, 64–67
other colleges/ universities, 70–71
planning, 57, 85–86
program review, 39, 41
social issues, 71
threats to innovation, 4
vulnerability to, 32–34
Exxon Education Foundation, 14, 20

F

Facility planning, 96
Faculty
barrier to change, 15, 16
consulting: encouragement of, 25
participation in planning, 55, 84–85
student ratio, 84
Federal student aid: decline, 32
Financial factors
decision making constraints, 74
fiscal exigency, 43
program/facility planning, 96
reallocation, 39, 40, 78, 79
success factor, 90, 92
Ford Foundation, 68
Foundations support, 68
Fragmentation: danger of, 94
Funding, 63
Futures committee, 66

Missouri State Coordinating Board, 45

N

A Nation at Risk, 29
National Center for Higher Education Management Systems, 60
National Endowment for the Humanities, 68
National Space Transportation System, 92
Needs assessment
    description, 59–60
    planning style, 54, 58–59
Nevada
    proposal format, 80
    reallocation, 78
New academic programs (see also Program development)
    corporate support, 69–70
    development processes, 86–87
    economic development, 67–68
    external needs/opportunities, 64–71
    foundation support, 68
    internal strengths, 52–64
    major considerations, 51–52
    scope of reviews, 79
    state support, 67–68
New Deal, 3
New Directions for Higher Education monograph series, 20
New Jersey
    Commission on Science and Technology, 68
    Department of Higher Education, 68
    "fast-track review," 84
    program approval, 80
New Mexico
    Commission on Higher Education, 83
    postapproval, 76
New York University, 63
"Niche," 35
Normative/reeducative change strategies, 22

O

Oklahoma State University, 63
Old Dominion University, 68
Open input (innovation strategy), 22–23
Organizational characteristics
    climate for innovation, 93
    cultural, 5–7
    during decline, 33
    flexibility, 31

impediments to innovation, 4
internal strengths, 52–64
size, 7–8, 12, 72
personnel, 93–94
stagnation, 34
structural, 7–14

P

Personnel variables, 7, 93–94
Planned linkage (innovation strategy), 23
Planning styles, 53–59, 90
Policies and Procedures for Six-Year Curricular Plans, 80
Politics
    decision making factors, 12
    obstacles to innovation, 13
    support building, 13–14
Portfolio analysis
    assumption, 43
    evaluation tool, 61, 62
    justification, 40
    matrix, 36, 38
    priority setting, 39
Postapproval, 76
Potential for change, 7
Power
    conflict, 12
    innovation strategy, 22, 23
    lack of as impediment, 6
Preapproval criteria, 92
Preproposal approval, 76, 77
Presidents, 16–17
Priority Fund (U. of Michigan), 62
Priority setting
    decision making, 71–74
    evaluation criteria, 43, 63, 64
    portfolio analysis, 39
Private colleges, 72, 79, 81
Problem solving
    participative, 22
    problem focused planning style, 54
Product development
    comparison with program development, 51–52
    decision making, 9
Product life cycle, 36, 43
Program approval
    literature on, 37

ASHE-ERIC HIGHER EDUCATION REPORTS

Since 1983, the Association for the Study of Higher Education (ASHE) and the ERIC Clearinghouse on Higher Education, a sponsored project of the School of Education and Human Development at the George Washington University, have cosponsored the ASHE-ERIC Higher Education Report series. The 1988 series is the seventeenth overall, with the American Association for Higher Education having served as cosponsor before 1983.

Each monograph is the definitive analysis of a tough higher education problem, based on thorough research of pertinent literature and institutional experiences. After topics are identified by a national survey, noted practitioners and scholars write the reports, with experts reviewing each manuscript before publication.

Eight monographs (10 monographs before 1985) in the ASHE-ERIC Higher Education Report series are published each year, available individually or by subscription. Subscription to eight issues is $60 regular; $50 for members of AERA, AAHE, and AIR; $40 for members of ASHE (add $10.00 for postage outside the United States).

Prices for single copies, including 4th class postage and handling, are $15.00 regular and $11.25 for members of AERA, AAHE, AIR, and ASHE ($10.00 regular and $7.50 for members for 1985 to 1987 reports, $7.50 regular and $6.00 for members for 1983 and 1984 reports, $6.50 regular and $5.00 for members for reports published before 1983). If faster postage is desired for U.S. and Canadian orders, add $1.00 for each publication ordered; overseas, add $5.00. For VISA and MasterCard payments, include card number, expiration date, and signature. Orders under $25 must be prepaid. Bulk discounts are available on orders of 15 or more reports (not applicable to subscriptions). Order from the Publications Department, ASHE-ERIC Higher Education Reports, The George Washington University, One Dupont Circle, Suite 630, Washington, D.C. 20036-1183, or phone us at 202/296-2597. Write for a publications list of all the Higher Education Reports available.

1988 ASHE-ERIC Higher Education Reports

1. The Invisible Tapestry: Culture in American Colleges and Universities
   George D. Kuh and Elizabeth J. Whitt

2. Critical Thinking: Theory, Research, Practice, and Possibilities
   Joanne Gainen Kurfiss

3. Developing Academic Programs: The Climate for Innovation
   Daniel T. Seymour

1987 ASHE-ERIC Higher Education Reports

1. Incentive Early Retirement Programs for Faculty: Innovative Responses to a Changing Environment
   Jay L. Chronister and Thomas R. Kepple, Jr.

2. Working Effectively with Trustees: Building Cooperative Campus Leadership
   Barbara E. Taylor

3. Formal Recognition of Employer-Sponsored Instruction: Conflict and Collegiality in Postsecondary Education
   Nancy S. Nash and Elizabeth M. Hawthorne

4. Learning Styles: Implications for Improving Educational Practices
   Charles S. Claxton and Patricia H. Murrell

5. Higher Education Leadership: Enhancing Skills through Professional Development Programs
   Sharon A. McDade

6. Higher Education and the Public Trust: Improving Stature in Colleges and Universities
   Richard L. Alfred and Julie Weissman

7. College Student Outcomes Assessment: A Talent Development Perspective
   Maryann Jacobi, Alexander Astin, and Frank Ayala, Jr.

8. Opportunity from Strength: Strategic Planning Clarified with Case Examples
   Robert G. Cope

1986 ASHE-ERIC Higher Education Reports

1. Post-tenure Faculty Evaluation: Threat or Opportunity?
   Christine M. Licata

2. Blue Ribbon Commissions and Higher Education: Changing Academe from the Outside
   Janet R. Johnson and Lawrence R. Marcus

3. Responsive Professional Education: Balancing Outcomes and Opportunities
   Joan S. Stark, Malcolm A. Lowther, and Bonnie M.K. Hagerty

4. Increasing Students' Learning: A Faculty Guide to Reducing Stress among Students
   Neal A. Whitman, David C. Spendlove, and Claire H. Clark

5. Student Financial Aid and Women: Equity Dilemma?
   Mary Moran

6. The Master's Degree: Tradition, Diversity, Innovation
   Judith S. Glazer

7. The College, the Constitution, and the Consumer Student: Implications for Policy and Practice
   Robert M. Hendrickson and Annette Gibbs

8. Selecting College and University Personnel: The Quest and the Questions
   Richard A. Kaplowitz

1985 ASHE-ERIC Higher Education Reports

1. Flexibility in Academic Staffing: Effective Policies and Practices
   Kenneth P. Mortimer, Marque Bagshaw, and Andrew T. Masland

2. Associations in Action: The Washington, D.C., Higher Education Community
   Harland G. Bloland

3. And on the Seventh Day: Faculty Consulting and Supplemental Income
   Carol M. Boyer and Darrell R. Lewis

4. Faculty Research Performance: Lessons from the Sciences and Social Sciences
   John W. Creswell

5. Academic Program Reviews: Institutional Approaches, Expectations, and

Controversies
Clifton F. Conrad and Richard F. Wilson

6. Students in Urban Settings: Achieving the Baccalaureate Degree
Richard C. Richardson, Jr., and Louis W. Bender

7. Serving More Than Students: A Critical Need for College Student Personnel Services
Peter H. Garland

8. Faculty Participation in Decision Making: Necessity or Luxury?
Carol E. Floyd

1984 ASHE-ERIC Higher Education Reports

1. Adult Learning: State Policies and Institutional Practices
K. Patricia Cross and Anne-Marie McCartan

2. Student Stress: Effects and Solutions
Neal A. Whitman, David C. Spendlove, and Claire H. Clark

3. Part-time Faculty: Higher Education at a Crossroads
Judith M. Gappa

4. Sex Discrimination Law in Higher Education: The Lessons of the Past Decade
J. Ralph Lindgren, Patti T. Ota, Perry A. Zirkel, and Nan Van Gieson

5. Faculty Freedoms and Institutional Accountability: Interactions and Conflicts
Steven G. Olswang and Barbara A. Lee

6. The High-Technology Connection: Academic/Industrial Cooperation for Economic Growth
Lynn G. Johnson

7. Employee Educational Programs: Implications for Industry and Higher Education
Suzanne W. Morse

8. Academic Libraries: The Changing Knowledge Centers of Colleges and Universities
Barbara B. Moran

9. Futures Research and the Strategic Planning Process: Implications for Higher Education
James L. Morrison, William L. Renfro, and Wayne I. Boucher

10. Faculty Workload: Research, Theory, and Interpretation
Harold E. Yuker

1983 ASHE-ERIC Higher Education Reports

1. The Path to Excellence: Quality Assurance in Higher Education
Laurence R. Marcus, Anita O. Leone, and Edward D. Goldberg

2. Faculty Recruitment, Retention, and Fair Employment: Obligations and Opportunities
John S. Waggaman

3. Meeting the Challenges: Developing Faculty Careers*
Michael C.T. Brookes and Katherine L. German

*Out-of-print. Available through EDRS.

*Out-of-print. Available through EDRS.